ESSAYS ON
INDIAN ART, INDUSTRY & EDUCATION

ESSAYS ON INDIAN ART, INDUSTRY & EDUCATION

E. B. HAVELL

GYAN

Published by

Gyan Publishing House
5, Ansari Road
Daryaganj, New Delhi-110002
Phone: 011-47034999, 9811692060
E-mail: books@gyanbooks.com

Distribution Network
gyanbooks.com
India, USA, Canada, UK, Australia, France

ISBN: 978-81-212-8802-6 (PB)
First Published, 1907

2nd Impression 2023

Printed at: Gyan Press, Delhi.

ESSAYS ON INDIAN ART, INDUSTRY & EDUCATION
Author: E. B. Havell

ESSAYS ON

INDIAN ART, INDUSTRY & EDUCATION.

BY

E. B. HAVELL.

Late Principal, Government School of Art,
and Keeper of the Government Art Gallery, Calcutta,
Author of "Indian Sculpture and Painting;"
"Benares: The Sacred City;"
"A Hand-Book to Agra and the Taj;" etc.

PUBLISHED BY

G. A. NATESAN & CO., ESPLANADE,

Madras.

PREFACE.

The various Essays on Indian Art, Industry, and Education which are here reprinted, though mostly written some years ago, all deal with questions which continue to possess a living interest. The superstitions which they attempt to dispel still loom largely in popular imagination, and the reforms they advocate still remain to be carried out. Only last year Sir Henry Craik, M. P., in his book on India, revived the familiar Anglo-Indian legend that the Taj Mahal was the creation of a European architect. Hardly any serious attempt has been made in the last twenty-five years to make the departmental machinery of Government effective for the revival of Indian art and handicraft. Officialism in the Calcutta University has lately barred the way to further progress in art education over-riding the deliberate vote of the majority of the members of the Senate. Swadeshi politicians, with regard to India's industrial problems, have been content to follow behind commercial Europe, and multiply the evils which the factory system has already inflicted upon India.

Knowing that the best artistic opinion of Europe is wholly on my side, and believing that the removal of departmental impediments to the progress of Indian art and industry are urgently called for, both for the sake of British prestige and in the interest of India herself, I offer no apology for putting my arguments before the Government and the public again and again, in season and out of season.

I have to thank the Editors of *The Nineteenth Century and After*; *The Calcutta Review*; and of *East and West*, Bombay, for the permission they have kindly given to reprint the Essays which originally appeared in those Reviews.

E. B. HAVELL.

PREFACE

CONTENTS.

THE TAJ AND ITS DESIGNERS.

ALL who have seen the great masterpiece of Indian architecture, the Taj at Agra, or know it by illustration and description, are familiar with the legends which ascribe its conception to the genius of some obscure Italian architect, and its exquisite inlaid decoration to Austin de Bordeaux, a French adventurer, who was employed for some years at the Court of Shah Jahan. The readiness with which the tradition has been accepted as history by European writers is comprehensible, for every European who gazes at the ethereal beauty of the Taj must feel some pride if he can bring himself to believe that the crowning glory of one of the most brilliant epochs of Indian art owed its inspiration to Western minds. Nevertheless, it must be confessed that the credence generally given to this vague romance does more credit to our imagination than to our historical sense, or artistic judgment. Indian art is still very little understood by Europeans. We feel and admire the decorative element in it, but deny to it higher imaginative qualities. The Indian art which we know and understand best is the least important part of it. It only comprises those accessories of Indian domestic life which, however beautiful they may sometimes be, lose all their artistic significance when detached from the surroundings for which they are intended, and invariably suffer artistically from the interest we take in them. We have been unable to follow the trend of Indian artistic thought beyond this decorative constituent quality, because from this point it becomes much more abstract and abstruse than our own. And no one will ever get further in his understanding and appreciation of Indian art without forsaking that stolid attitude of ignorant condescension with which the ordinary European, and more especially the Anglo-Saxon, treats everything Oriental which he does not understand. If, throwing aside pre-conceived notions and insular prejudices, we approach Indian art with the same spirit as animated the European pioneers of Sanskrit research, we shall like them find ourselves revelling in new fields of wonder and beauty, the fairyland of Eastern romance and poetry. We should then see how ridiculous we, and the educated Indians who follow our example, make ourselves by importing European pictures and sculpture in the belief that we are thereby throwing a flood of Western light upon the darkness of the East. The spirituality of Indian art permeates the whole of it, but it shines brightest at the point where we cease to see and understand it.

Everything connected with the history of the Taj is important to the student of Indian art, for the Taj is the consummation of a great artistic development, the traditions of which remain alive even at the present day. The truth or otherwise of the legends I have referred to is of cardinal importance, for if it be accepted that an Italian or French artist designed the masterpiece of the Mogul epoch, there would be much force in the theory that the Indian requires the aid of a higher Western intelligence to perfect his artistic ideas. Let us then consider carefully the historical and artistic grounds on which those traditions rest. The circumstances which led to the building of the Taj are well known and need not be given in detail. The death in childbed of Mumtaz Mahal—'the Crown of the Palace' —Shah Jahan's favourite wife in A. D. 1629; the distracted grief of the Emperor and his resolve to build her a monument which should be one of the wonders of the world. He sent for all the best architects of his Empire, in consultation with whom he inspected and rejected many hundreds of designs. At last one design was accepted, a model of it was made in wood, and from this model the Taj was built.

So far all accounts agree. But as to the name of the

architect selected we have, on the one hand, the unanimous statements of contemporary Indian writers, and on the other, a story related by a Spanish priest, Father Manrique, who visited Agra ten years after the Taj was begun. The former agree that the design was made by Ustad Isa, a celebrated architect who, according to one account (preserved in the Imperial Library, Calcutta), came from Shiraz, and according to others, from *Rum*, which may mean either Constantinople or some part of Asiatic Turkey. The style of the Taj points to the probability that his native place was Shiraz, though it is quite possible that he may have been employed by the Sultan of Turkey at Constantinople. Father Manrique in his description of the Taj, then under construction, relates the following story, told to him by Father Da Castro of Lahore, who was the executor of of the will the obscure Italian who thus claimed to have designed the Taj:

> The architect was a Venetian, named Geronimo Verroneo, who came to India with the ships of the Portuguese, and who died at Lahore a little before my arrival. Of him a report was current that the Padsha, having sent for him and made known to him the desire he felt to build there (at Agra) a sumptuous and grandiose monument to his defunct consort, the architect Verroneo obeyed, and in a few days produced various models of very fine architecture, showing all the skill of his art; also that, having contented his Majesty in this, he dissatisfied him—according to his barbarous and arrogant pride—by the modesty of his estimates; further that, growing angry, he ordered him to spend three krors, and to let him know when they were spent.

Now in estimating the comparative historical value of these two versions it must be allowed that the absence of any mention of Verroneo in the contemporary Indian accounts does not necessarily discredit his story, for it is well known that Muhammedan writers often omitted from their works any facts which might bring honour to their religious opponents. On the other hand, Verroneo's story contains so many of the wildest improbabilities that it is extraordinary that Anglo-Indian writers should have accepted it with so little hesitation. In the first place, it is necessary to consider that in the type of adventurers 'who came with the ships of the Portugüese' to India in the seventeenth century and entered the service of the Great Mogul, one would not expect to find the transcendent artistic genius such as the designer of the Taj possessed. Bernier, the French physician, who resided several years at the Mogul Court during the reign of Aurangzebe, incidentally throws a side-light on their character in his description of the famous Peacock Throne, a part of which was designed by a Frenchman (supposed to be Austin de Bordeaux) who, 'having circumvented many Princes of Europe with his false gems, which he knew to make admirably well, fled to the Mogul Court where he made his fortune.' Verroneo seems to have been less successful in the latter respect, but he certainly contrived to emulate Austin in making for himself a fictitious fame, which has lasted to the present day. At the time when the Taj was built the position of the Franks, as Europeans were called, was by no means what it was in the days of Akbar and Jahangir, the two preceding Emperors. They were mostly employed in the artillery or in the arsenals, and Bernier tells us that in his time they were admitted with difficulty into the service; and that, whereas formerly, when the Moguls were little skilled in the management of artillery they received as much as two hundred rupees a month and upwards, their pay was now limited to thirty-two rupees. The Jesuits, who had enjoyed great favour under his father and grandfather, were bitterly persecuted by Shah Jahan. He deprived them of their pension, destroyed the Church at Lahore and the greater part of that of Agra, demolishing a steeple which contained a clock heard in every part of the City. Only a short time before her death Mumtaz Mahal, who was a relentless enemy of the Christians, had instigated Shah Jahan to attack the Portuguese settlement at Hooghly. After a desperate resistance the Portuguese were overwhelmed. Two thousand, including women and children, took refuge on a warship and perished with the crew, as the Captain blew up the vessel rather than surrender.

Five hundred prisoners, among them some Jesuit priests, were sent to Agra. With threats of torture the Empress endeavoured to persuade the priests to renounce their religion. On their refusal they were thrown into prison, but after some months they were released and deported to the main Portuguese settlement at Goa. Their books, pictures, and images were destroyed by orders of Mumtaz Mahal. Her hatred for the Christians is perpetuated on her tomb in the mausoleum itself, which bears the significant inscription, 'Defend us from the tribe of unbelievers!' From Bernier we learn that no Christian was allowed inside the mausoleum, lest its sanctity be profaned.

In the face of these facts it would require the very strongest corroboration of Verroneo's story to make it credible that Shah Jahan, whose lifelong devotion to his wife was the strongest trait in his character, had chosen one of these hated unbelievers to be the chief designer of her monument. As a matter of fact Father Manrique's account is entirely uncorroborated by any other contemporary European writer. Neither Tavernier, who saw the commencement and completion of the Taj, nor Bernier, make any mention of Verroneo, or suggest that the building was in any way the work of a European. Bernier, in his description of it, expressly implies that he looked upon the Taj as a purely

Indian conception, for he naïvely confesses that though he thought 'that the extraordinary fabric could not be sufficiently admired,' he would not have ventured to express his opinion if it had not been shared in by his companion (Tavernier), for he feared that his taste might have been corrupted by his long residence in the Indies, and it was quite a relief to his mind to hear Tavernier say that he had seen nothing in Europe so bold and majestic. Thévenot, who saw the Taj in 1666, affirms that this superb monument is sufficient to show that the Indians are not ignorant of architecture; and though the style may appear curious to Europeans, it is in good taste, and though it is different from Greek or other ancient art, one can only say that it is very fine. The absence of any reference to Verroneo in the accounts of these three minute and impartial chroniclers of the Mogul times is very strong evidence that his story was partly or wholly a fabrication; otherwise it is impossible to believe that they would not have known and mentioned the fact that the chief architect was a European. Verroneo's finishing touch regarding the spending of 'three krors' is in itself suspicious. If he really had been in such a position his fame would have been known far and wide among his fellow-Europeans, for it was only the highest nobles of the Court who were entrusted with the expenditure on the construction of the principal Mogul buildings. The *Badshah Nama* mentions the names of the two nobles who actually superintended the building of the Taj—Makramat Khan and Mir Abdul Karim.

Father Manrique and the three writers I have mentioned are the only Europeans who have recorded contemporary knowledge of important facts connected with the Taj. It is unnecessary to refer to later accounts, borrowed more or less from them. While history affords practically no evidence in support of Verroneo's claim to immortal distinction, the Taj itself is the most convincing proof of the impudence of the assumption. The plan follows closely that of Humayun's Tomb, built by Akbar nearly a century earlier. Neither in general conception nor in the smallest detail does it suggest the style of the Italian Renaissance, which a Venetian architect of the seventeenth century would certainly have followed. If Verroneo's design had been executed we should doubtless have had some kind of Orientalised version of the Church of Santa Maria della Salute at Venice, instead of the Taj. It is inconceivable tha Shah Jahan, a man of cultivated artistic taste, surrounded as he was by all the most accomplished architects of the East, would have engaged a European to design a building in a purely Eastern style.

The Indian records relating to the Taj are unusually precise and detailed in the information they give with regard to the architects and workmen. The artistic history of the period, and the style and workmanship of the Taj, all testify in a remarkable way to their accuracy and the improbability of the theory that Europeans directed the design of the building. The places given in the Calcutta Imperial Library manuscript as the native towns of the principal architects and decorators—namely, Shiraz, Baghdad, and Samarkand—indicate precisely that part of Asia which was the cradle of the art represented by the Taj. The mention of Samarkand is especially interesting, for it is known that Tamerlane, after his invasion of India in A. D. 1398, carried off all the masons who had built the famous Mosque at Ferozabad (since destroyed), in order that they might build another like it at Samarkand. Most probably they were the descendants of those masons who came back to India to build the Taj.

Before dismissing Verroneo's story, it will be interesting to analyse it in order to separate the truth which may be in it from the falsehood. It is highly probable that Verroneo was one of the many architects who submitted designs for the Taj. His were doubtless in the style of the Renaissance, which was then the architectural style of Italy. Shah Jahan examined them with curiosity and expressed some qualified praise, which Verroneo mistook for approval. The anger of the Padsha on hearing of the estimates and his order 'to spend three krors' clearly point to the indirect Oriental method of rejecting a proposal, and it is quite certain that Verroneo heard nothing more of his commission from Shah Jahan. He returned to Lahore and poured the garbled account of his doings into the too credulous ears of Father Da Castro, who retailed it as history to his fellow-priest.

Father Manrique is also responsible for the statement that Augustin, or Austin de Bordeaux, was employed in the 'internal decorations' of the Taj. Hitherto every European writer has taken this to mean that Austin superintended the magnificent inlaid work technically known as *pietra dura*, which is the most striking feature in the decoration of the building, external and internal. There is a good deal of plausibility in the theory, though most authorities have been puzzled by the manifest inconsistencies which tell against it. At the back of the Throne Chamber in the Dîwan-i-am at Delhi there is a large piece of very realistic *pietra dura* work, undoubtedly Florentine in style. But, except for the silly chatter of native guides, who used to point out the panel of Orpheus as the portrait of Austin himself, there is not a vestige of historical evidence to connect him with it. Fergusson has shown that this panel (lately brought back from South Kensington and restored to its place by Lord Curzon) is a traditional Italian rendering of the classical story which can be traced back as far as to the catacombs at Rome. Sir George Birdwood, however, in his *Industrial Arts of India*, accepts the theory that Austin was responsible for the Taj decorations, as well as for the *pietra dura* work at Delhi, though in a later article in the *Journal of Indian Art* he says that 'it is quite impossible that the men who devised such artistic monstrosities (the Delhi panels) could have been the same as those whose hands traced in variegated *pietra dura* the exquisite arabesques of the Taj.'

Whoever the designer may have been, it is certain that the Delhi *pietra dura* was directed by some fourth-rate European artist. They are just as ill-adapted and out of harmony with the place they occupy, as the Taj decorations are marvellously contrived to beautify it. It is impossible to explain away the inconsistency of attributing the authorship of the magnificent Taj decorations, which are, as Sir George Birdwood says, 'strictly Indian of the Mogul period,' and the commonplace Florentine work at Delhi to one and the same person. This statement of Father Manrique can be explained in another and much more satisfactory way. We know from Tavernier that Austin was a silversmith, for he mentions that Shah Jahan had intended to employ him in covering with silver the vault of a great gallery in the palace at Agra. The French jeweller mentioned by Bernier in connection with the Peacock Throne is generally supposed to be Austin. Now the Taj originally possessed two silver doors, said to have cost 127,000 rupees, which were taken away and melted down when the Jâts sacked Agra. Before the existing marble screen was erected, the sarcophagus of the Empress was surrounded by a fence of solid gold, studded with gems. Surely the obvious and most satisfactory explanation of Austin's connection with the 'internal decorations' of the Taj is that he was occupied with gold and silver work? Such work would be part of the internal decoration, and yet it would have been executed outside, so that the sanctity of the tomb would not have been profaned by an unbeliever. Why should we make a French jeweller, goldsmith, and silversmith responsible for Italian and Indian *pietra dura* work, when there were both jewellers' work and gold and silver work on which he might have been employed?

In my opinion the Delhi *pietra dura* has been wrongly attributed to Shah Jahan's reign. It has all the appearance of eighteenth century work, and, as far as I am aware, there is no evidence worth considering to show that it existed previous to the reign of Aurangzebe. It could not have been executed in the latter reign, because the naturalistic representations of birds and animals was a violation of Musalman law, and would not have been permitted by that bigoted monarch. If the date ascribed to it is correct, it is more than astonishing that Aurangzebe, who mutilated all such representations at Fatehpur Sikri, should have spared them at the back of his own throne in the Delhi palace, for an old drawing, still in existence, shows that most of the inlay was in a good state of preservation down to 1837. It would certainly coincide with all the probabilities of the case to attribute it to one of the later Mogul Emperors, or the early part of the eighteenth century.

If we dismiss from our minds all these obscure and inconsistent legends about Austin de Bordeaux, it will be quite easy to see that the inlaid work of the Taj was the natural consummation of a great artistic movement purely Oriental in character, initiated by Akbar, the progression of which can be traced in existing Mogul buildings. Arabian workmen first introduced mosaic work into India. The kind of mosaic generally practised by the Arabs was tesselated work, technically known as *Alexandrinum opus,* which consisted of thin pieces of marble, coloured stones, glass, or enamelled tiles cut into geometric patterns, and closely fitted so as to cover the surface of a wall or floor. The technical difference between this and *pietra dura,* or true mosaic, is the difference between overlay and inlay. The Arab buildings were generally of brick, and the original intention of the mosaic was to give a surface of more precious material to a building of brick or common stone. The preference of the Arabs for geometric patterns is explained by two reasons: First, the Arabs belonged to the Sunni, or orthodox sect of Musalmans, observing the strict letter of the law which forbade the representation of 'the likeness of anything which is in heaven above, or in the earth beneath.' Secondly, the geometric design lent itself admirably to the character of the materials employed, and to the speedy and effective covering of a surface by this process. Now when the Arabs, or those who had learnt from them, began to work on buildings constructed chiefly of marble or fine stone, the *inlaid* work would naturally take the place of the other, because it would be superfluous and inartistic to decorate marble or stone with an *overlay* of the same material. Again, when the Arabian art of the orthodox Sunni school came into close connection with the unorthodox Shia, or naturalistic school of Persia, we should certainly expect to find representations of natural forms taking the place of geometric patterns. These are exactly the conditions which prevailed in India in the century which preceded the building of the Taj. Even long before that time, in the oldest Saracenic mausoleum in India, the tomb of Altamsh, which belongs to the thirteenth century, the red sandstone of the walls is inlaid with geometric tiles of white marble. In the buildings of Fatehpur Sikri (date about 1571 A. D.) we find frequent examples of overlay and not a few of inlay. A little later, in the gateway of Akbar's tomb at Sikandra, inlaid work is extensively used, though as yet still confined to geometric patterns. But twenty years afterwards, in the tomb of the Persian adventurer, Itmad-ud-daulah, the grandfather of Mumtaz Mahal, at Agra, the style is so far technically perfected that the inlaid work not only includes elaborate scrolls of conventional Arabian design, but the familiar *motifs* of Persian painted decoration, such as rosewater vessels, the cypress, the tree of life, and various other flower forms. The date of this building is about A. D 1622.

The similiar progression from geometric to naturalistic forms may be traced in Italian mosaic. But the synchronous development of two similar schools in Italy and in India is nothing more than one of those coincidences which often lead historians to wrong conclusions. The later Italian inlayers imitated the work of Italian fresco and oil painters. The Indian inlayers likewise imitated the work of the Persian artists who founded the Indian school of painting of the Mogul period. The step from the Itmad-ud-daulah to the Taj is simply the change from a conventional school of Persian painting to a more developed and more realistic one. This is only what we might expect if we remember Shah Jahan's resolve that the Taj should surpass every other building in the world. That there was a strong naturalistic tendency in the Indian painting of the Mogul period is known to all who have studied this interesting phase of Mogul art. It is very clearly shown in a series of exquisite miniature paintings of Jahangir's time, now in the Government Art Gallery, Calcutta, which I fortunately rescued from the unappreciative hands of a Muhammedan bookseller a few years ago. They include portraits of the nobles of Jahangir's Court and some studies of Indian birds, drawn and painted with a fidelity and delicacy which would do credit to a Japanese master. On one of them, sealed and signed by Jahangir himself, there is a note, written by the Emperor, to the effect that it was painted by Ustad Mansur, 'the most celebrated painter of this time,' in the nineteenth year of his reign (A. D. 1624, six years before the Taj was begun). The borders of three of these paintings are ornamented with floral designs which, making allowance for the different technical treatment required by a different material, are of the exact type of the Taj decorations. No one who studies these remarkable paintings and compares them with the floral decoration of the Taj would hesitate to say that it was the work of this Persian school, and not any European model, that the Indian mosaic workers were imitating. It might possibly have been these same paintings, prized so much by his father, that Shah Jahan gave as patterns to the workmen.

No doubt it is true that here and there in Mogul art one meets with a detail which suggests European influence. It was a time of great artistic activity, and in such times any living art which comes into contact with another exchanges ideas with it. But the European element in the Mogul style is far less strongly marked than is the Oriental in Italian art. During the whole period of Italy's close commercial intercourse with the East, her art and industries were very strongly impressed with Oriental ideas. It would be easy to find in Italian art a dozen instances just as striking as the similarity (which is a similarity of technique and not of style) between the *pietra dura* of Florence and that of the

Taj. No one suggests, on that account, that Indian artists came to Italy to instruct the Italians.

It is probable that long before the building of Itmad-ud-daulah's tomb the art of inlaying had been learnt by Hindu workmen and become absorbed into Indian art through that wonderful power of assimilation which Hinduism has always shown. Some Indian records of the Taj mention the name of one Mannu Beg, from *Rum*, as the principal mosaic worker; but, in the list of the principal workmen given by the Imperial Library manuscript, five mosaic workers from Kanauj, all with Hindu names, are entered. That they were artists of great reputation may be gathered from the fact that their salaries ranged from 200 rupees to 800 rupees a month. The best Agra mosaic workers of the present day are also Hindus, and in many parts of northern India the artistic traditions of the Moguls are still kept alive by Hindu workmen.

The Mogul style is a symphony of artistic ideas formed into an interchanging harmony by the fusion of Hindu thought with the art of the two rival sects of Muhammedanism, the Sunni and the Shia. Ruskin's criticism of Mogul architecture as an 'evanescent style' is a very superficial one. The great development of Mogul art represented by the Taj died out because during Aurangzebe's long reign the bigotry of the

Sunni sect was in the ascendant, and the Shia and Hindu artists were banished from the Mogul Court. But before Aurangzebe's accession the traditions of Mogul architecture were firmly established in the more distant parts of his dominions, and there they survive to this day, absorbed into the great synthesis of Indian art, and only prevented from continuing their natural evolution through the fatal want of artistic understanding which has made the dead styles of Europe the official architecture of India.

The Taj has been the subject of numberless critical essays, but many of them have missed the mark entirely, because the writers have not been sufficiently conversant with the spirit of Eastern artistic thought. All comparisons with the Parthenon or other classic buildings are useless. One cannot compare Homer with the Mahâbhârata, or Kalidâs with Euripides. The Parthenon was a temple for Pallas Athene, an exquisite casket to contain the jewel. The Taj is the jewel—the ideal itself. Indian architecture is in much closer affinity to the great conceptions of the Gothic builders than it is to anything of classic or Renaissance construction. The Gothic Cathedral, with its sculptured arches and its spires pointing heavenwards, is a symbol, as most Eastern buildings are symbols. But the Taj stands alone among Eastern buildings: for it represents in art the same effort towards individualism, the struggle against the restraints of ritualism and dogma which Akbar initiated in religion.

Every one who has seen the Taj must have felt that there is something in it, difficult to define or analyse, which differentiates it from all other buildings in the world. Sir Edwin Arnold has struck the true note of criticism in the following lines :

> Not architecture ! as all others are,
> But the proud passion of an Emperor's love
> Wrought into living stone, which gleams and soars
> With body of beauty shrining soul and thought ;
> . . . . as when some face
> Divinely fair unveils before our eyes—
> Some woman beautiful unspeakably—
> And the blood quickens, and the spirit leaps,
> And will to worship bends the half-yielded knees,
> While breath forgets to breathe. So is the Taj.

This is not a mere flight of poetic fancy, but a deep and true interpretation of the meaning of the Taj. What were the thoughts of the designers, and of Shah Jahan himself, when they resolved to raise a monument of eternal love to the Crown of the Palace—Taj Mahal ? Surely not only of a mausoleum—a sepulchre fashioned after ordinary architectural canons, but of an architectonic ideal, symbolical of her womanly grace and beauty. Those critics who have objected to the effeminacy of the architecture unconsciously pay the highest tribute to the genius of the builders. The Taj was meant to be feminine. The whole conception, and every line and detail of it, express the intention of the designers. It is Mumtaz Mahal herself, radiant in her youthful beauty, who still lingers on the banks of the shining Jumna, at early morn, in the glowing mid-day sun, or in the silver moonlight! Or rather, we should say it conveys a more abstract thought, it is India's noble tribute to the grace of Indian womanhood—the Venus de Milo of the East.

To the art student nothing can be more fascinating than the endeavour to analyse the artistic thoughts of different countries and different races. But England as a nation has a concern in trying to understand Indian ideals. For it is neither by railways and canals, sanitation and police, coal-mines and gold-mines, factories and mills, nor by English text-books, and the real or imaginary fusion of Western and Eastern culture, that we shall build for ourselves a permanent Indian Empire. Nor should we flatter ourselves that British justice is creating in India a lasting sense of gratitude for British rule. The very uprightness of our rule is slowly but surely creating an Indian question which, though it seems smaller than a man's hand to-day, may fill the Eastern horizon to-morrow. When India has grown out of its political infancy it will yearn for something more than just laws and regulations. India is governed by ideas, not by principles or by statutes. Concrete justice, as represented by the complicated machinery of the British law, is to the Indian a gamble in which the longest purses and most successful liars win. Abstract justice, as it was personified in the Great Queen, the mother of her people, touches India to the quick. That one idea has done more for Indian loyalty than all the text-books of the Universities or Acts of the Governor-General in Council. It was only an idea that roused India in 1857, and before an idea which touched the profounder depths of Indian sentiment all the Western culture in which we believe might be swept away as dust before a cyclone and leave not a trace behind.—*Nineteenth Century and After, June, 1903.*

THE REVIVAL OF INDIAN HANDICRAFT.*

I

The industrial development of India is a question which has so many aspects—each of which can be viewed from a great many different standpoints—that it is hardly surprising to find a great dissimilarity in the opinion and judgment of different authorities. In these circumstances it is wise to distrust those who, with loud voice, proclaim a sure and simple solution of all the difficulties of the subject, and, on the other hand, we must avoid the even greater danger of believing that a *laissez faire*, or let-things-alone policy is the only possible one. For the public it is more important to obtain a general idea of the direction in which progress may be expected and to understand the evil effects which may come from taking a wrong direction, than to attempt to enter into technical details which only experts can properly appreciate. So I will not in this lecture inflict upon you many technical details. The industrial development of a country depends partly on

* A lecture delivered before the Indian Industrial Association, July 1901.

the state of its natural resources, partly on its geographical situation and physical characteristics, partly on political advantages or disadvantages, and partly on its manufacturing capacity. England's present commercial prosperity has been founded partly on her natural wealth of coal, iron, china-clay, and other raw materials for manufacture; partly on her position as the great carrying power of the world, partly on the inventive genius of her artisans, which gave her the start of other countries in mechanical industry.

In natural resources, and physical and geographical advantages, India is certainly very richly endowed. Politically, India is a partner in the great British Empire—a position which secures for her at least the internal peace, justice, and settled government which are the foundation-stones of all commercial prosperity. It is, chiefly, in her position as a manufacturing country that India has lost ground in the last two centuries. Now I do not propose to make more than a passing allusion to the exploitation of the natural resources of India, because, in the first place, it is a subject large enough in itself for many lectures, and secondly, because the ways and means of it are not so much the subject of controversy as other questions are. Progress in this direction will always be slow, until scientific and technical education in this country have advanced beyond the theoretic smattering required for academic degrees into the higher plane of sure and practical knowledge, which is generally only reached after academic distinctions are won; and until some means have been discovered to make the field more attractive to private enterprise and capital than it is at present.

A great difficulty, no doubt, is that native capital generally finds highly profitable and safe investments in long-established traditional grooves, from which it is loath to depart for the less known and less certain ways of modern scientific exploitation. I would only venture to observe that the self-reliant character of Englishmen and the traditional policy of England perhaps incline us to expect too much of private enterprise in India. Private enterprise in this country has not yet acquired the same robust and independent constitution as it has in Europe or in the great English Colonies. Neither has the glowing prospectus of the Company-promoter quite the same power of attracting capital in India as it has in London and other great financial centres. The recognition of these conditions may be seen in the guarantees for railways and other means by which the paternal Government tries to put more heart into the timid Indian investor; but when we observe the much more strenuous official support which is given to private enterprise in most European countries and in

America, I venture to think it would be well for India if we departed a little more from our traditional policy in this matter.

I will pass over geographical, physical and political aspects of the question, and come to the main point I wish to deal with, namely, the development of the manufacturing capacity of India. We know that in former times this country held a commanding position in the textile industries of the world. India not only supplied all her own wants in textiles, but had a very flourishing export trade. We know also that India has lost that position though improvements made in textile apparatus and machinery by European weavers, above all, by the application of steam power to textile manufacture. Now I have continually noticed that the moral which most people draw from the history of the development of European manufactures is that if India is to regain its position as a great manufacturing country, it must follow in the footsteps of European industry, revolutionise the working conditions of its traditional handicrafts, turn the village workshops into steam factories, and give up hand labour for mechanical power. They start on the assumption that India's salvation depends on her artisans joining in the great competition for export markets, which is going on in Europe and America. They take it for granted that processes which have become necessary in Europe must also be necessary in India, where totally different conditions prevail.

If these two assumptions were correct, I fear the prospect for India would not be very bright. I think no friend of India could view with unconcern the prospect of a coming era of congested cities and depopulated rural districts, of unhealthy conditions of work, of struggles between capital and labour, uneven distribution of wealth, social unrest and all the attendant evils of the great industrial development in Europe and America. Besides, the Indian artizan is unfitted both by disposition and habits from entering upon such a struggle, and generations must elapse before he could acquire, not only the technical knowledge, but the business methods and business capacity necessary for success in an industrial struggle in European markets. The Japanese, on the other hand, who seem to be preparing to compete in European markets with European methods, are far better equipped in all respects than Indian artisans. They are more self-reliant, they have generally much greater technical skill, greater capacity for adapting themselves to different methods of work, more enterprise and determination. I venture to prophesy that unless India rouses herself to greater efforts in industrial improvement, she will find Japan a more formidable commercial and industrial competitor than either Europe or America. China, too, if she should one day wake from her long sleep, could put into the field an army of highly skilled, patient, industrious workmen which could defeat the Indian artisan at almost every point.

The idea that the handicraftsmen of India must look abroad to foreign markets, of whose requirements they are totally ignorant, when there are over 300,000,000 customers at their own doors whose wants they know and understand, seems to me altogether illogical. First let them struggle to recover the home markets they have lost. If they succeed in that they may possibly acquire the skill and knowledge necessary for attempting the other. If they do not succeed in one enterprise, in which all the advantages are on their side, is it likely they will win in another in which they will have to face every disadvantage? But, you may ask, is it possible that Indian workmen can stand against foreign competition without copying foreign methods of trade and manufacture? That is one of those questions which cannot be answered by a simple 'yes' or 'no.' It depends upon circumstances. But I will assert this, that those who believe that hand labour in manufacture is becoming a thing of the past are entertaining a delusion fatal to real progress in

India. Nowhere in the world is there a more splendid field for the development of hand industries than there is in India. If the same amount of thought, enterprise, and capital had been spent during the last 50 years in developing the handicrafts of India as have been spent in establishing mills and factories on the European system, I do not hesitate to affirm that India would have been richer by crores and crores of rupees, and we should hear little to-day of the decline of Indian industries.

Hand manufactures can be developed and improved quite as much as mechanical industry. A country like India, which possesses hundreds of thousands of skilled handicraftsmen, and where the cost of living is many times cheaper than it is in Europe, possesses a source of potential wealth capable of almost indefinite expansion.

It is the most suicidal and fatuous policy to assume that the skilled Indian handicraftsman must be turned into a cooly minding a machine. Yet this is the policy which many people seriously put forward as the only means of reviving Indian industry.

Now I will leave theoretical discussion and enter into practical details. There are one or two points in the present condition of the Indian textile industry to which I should like to draw your special attention.

The first is that though the hand-looms used in India to-day are the same as have been used for hundreds of generations, and hardly any attempt has ever been made to improve them, yet the Indian hand-loom industry has by no means been entirely crushed by all the marvellous skill which has been brought to bear upon the construction of the European power-loom. No doubt it is in a very depressed condition, but it is still, next to agriculture, the most important of Indian industries. Two-thirds of the skilled artisan population of India are, at the present day, hand-loom weavers, and the value of the annual outturn of hand-woven fabrics is a matter of crores of rupees. We know that the very keen competition between European manufactures has reduced their profits to a comparatively small margin. If, then, the mechanical efficiency of the Indian hand-loom could be improved, say by 15 per cent., which would be equivalent to a 15 per cent. duty on the imports of foreign piece-goods, it is reasonable to suppose that the Indian weaver might retrieve his position to a very large extent.

Now it is not only probable but an indisputable fact that the ordinary Indian hand-loom can be easily made more effective, not merely by 15 per cent., but by nearly 100 per cent. There are many kinds of hand-looms in use in India, from a primitive arrangement of a few sticks to the elaborate and ingenious apparatus used for Benares kincobs and textiles of a similar class. The loom of the ordinary kind, or that used for cotton cloths of medium quality, is mechanically as effective an apparatus as the European hand-loom was 150 years ago, at a time when the Indian weaver not only had it all his own way in India, but was a formidable competitor in the European market. But since that time, while the Indian loom has remained the same, the European hand-weaver, by simple contrivances, which cost very little, has improved his loom in efficiency by nearly 100 per cent. The chief of these improvements is called the "fly-shuttle," a simple but ingenious arrangement by which the shuttle, instead of being thrown by hand, is jerked across the warp by pulling a string attached to a lever. It was invented by an English weaver about the middle of the 18th century, and the discovery gave to England the supremacy in the textile markets of the world—a position she has maintained since. It has always been a matter of astonishment to me that after a lapse of a century and-a-half this invention is almost unknown in India outside the great mills, where the principle of it is applied to the power-loom. The sewing machine, which is a much more recent invention, is known in almost every Indian village. There are goldsmiths and jewellers, brass-smiths, blacksmiths, and carpenters, all over India, who use European labour-saving appliances and improved tools, but practically nothing has hitherto been done for the improvement of the most important of all Indian handicrafts. European ladies have introduced the sewing machine, European firms and workshops have taught the goldsmith, brass-smith, blacksmith and carpenter; no one has hitherto helped the Indian weaver and he has not, like his European fellow-workman, been able to help himself.

In the Madras Presidency, where I have inspected thousands of native hand-looms, I never discovered a fly-shuttle, except in the Basel Mission weaving establishments and a few other Mission schools. The use of it never seems to spread among the weavers outside. A short time ago I discovered, through a Report written by Mr. Collin in 1890, that it was used by a prosperous colony of weavers in the Hughli and adjacent districts, chiefly at Serampore. How they came to adopt it I could not ascertain, but probably some one, during the time of the Danish Government at Serampore, had imported a European hand-loom and taught the weavers how to use it. You will be glad to hear that the Bengal Government, at my suggestion, are taking steps to make the use of the fly-shuttle known, throughout the Province. At present it is in partial use in 8 districts out of the 48. No doubt long and patient efforts will have to be made to persuade the mass of the weaving population to overcome their dislike to innovations, even though the benefits to be derived from them may be obvious. I would strongly recommend that the Indian Industrial Association should make this a prominent part of their programme. Your Association could easily form local Committees to assist and supplement Government efforts. If you succeed, as I am sure you would succeed, in bringing the fly-shuttle into general use among the weavers of Bengal, you would do a great service to your country.

The mechanical improvement of hand-looms is, in my opinion, one of the most important industrial problems to be dealt with in India, and perhaps one of those which present the least difficulties. I only hope that other Governments will follow the lead of Bengal in this matter, and that District Boards and Municipalities all over the country will assist in reviving the great Indian hand-loom industry. It is my firm belief that there is hardly a more safe and lucrative field open for Native and European capitalists in India than there is in the development of hand-loom weaving. Hand-loom factories are profitable in Europe; they should be much more so in India, where conditions are so much more favourable. It is commonly believed in India that the hand-loom industry in Europe has been entirely supplanted by the power-loom. This is very far from being the case. In France, Switzerland, and Italy there is still a great deal of silk weaving done by hand. In Scandinavia, you will find the hand-loom in every village, and the peasant women will not only weave their own linen, but spin the thread they require for sewing. In England, the great centre of the power-loom industry, there has been lately a remarkable revival of hand-loom weaving. Hand-loom factories are being established in many places, where formerly everything was done by the power-loom. The demand for skilled weavers is greater than the supply. I should like to read you a few extracts from a lecture given by Miss Clive Bayley, before the Society of Arts, London, a few years ago: "The recrudescence of the silk trade in the hand branches has drawn its workers away from the congested city streets into the purer air and cheaper regions of Suffolk and Essex. Ipswich, Braintree, Sudbury, and the villages round are becoming centres of renewed activity, and if you want hand-weavers you will find it pretty well impossible to get them. . . .

"Given the possibility of obtaining good weavers in the silk trade, the proceeds of a hand factory are quite as great as those of a steam factory. The outlay in machinery in the latter instance is far greater than in the former. The time and labour of getting the machinery under weigh is for short lengths far more in a power-loom than in a hand-loom, and the work of intricate patterns is infinitely superior when placed in the hands of a practised weaver than when entrusted to automatic machinery. Hand-loom firms rarely fail—power-loom firms are not nearly, I am told, so fortunate in this respect. But the great deficiency is workers; for after the first conquest of machinery the product of hand-labour was discounted, and the exaggerated importance and value of time seemed to paralyse industry." . . . .

"The superiority of work in the hand-looms will be a matter of positive proof and can be and is generally becoming a subject of interest. The better the class of hand-workers we train, the greater will be this difference, and the more potent will be the industrial revival which re-conquers what was supposed to be an abrogated kingdom." . . . . .

"One large silk firm is already raising the roof of its establishment in order to accommodate a large number of such hand working apprentices. Another applied, though for what exact purpose I have not discovered, for 500 similar workers. Another, and I believe a linen firm, was reported to need 2,000 workers." . . . "We have, however, barely touched on that all-important point—wages. What can a hand-weaver earn? As a matter of fact a hand-weaver is paid better than the watcher of machinery labour. He is also better paid now than at the end of the last century."

If the hand-loom can compete with the power-loom in England, where the cost of skilled labour is many times greater than it is in India, where the supply of trained weavers is very limited, and where the most perfect weaving machinery, worked by steam and electricity, is in use, what a much greater prospect must there be for it in India, where you have an unlimited supply of the most skilful hereditary weavers, content with earnings of three annas to eight annas a day!

I do not wish you to imagine that hand-weaving can hold its own against the power-loom to an unlimited extent. Both hand-labour and machinery have their limitations. But there are splendid possibilities open for the hand-loom industry in India, and it is a preventible loss to India that the skilled weavers should day by day leave their looms and add to the already overgrown agricultural population.

With proper looms and proper instruction the Indian weaver could not only recover a deal of the lost internal trade, but take a leading position in the world in hand-woven fabrics.

There are many branches of native industry in which simple mechanical improvements and labour-saving devices can be introduced, by means of which production can be increased or improved to a very large extent. But as I do not wish to enter into too many technical details, I will only allude to one other. Every one who is familiar with native brass-work knows how all the vessels, lamps and other things made by the process of casting, or, by the native method, laboriously moulded by hand in wax patterns which are destroyed in the casting, so that only one object can be cast from one pattern. This process is also used in Europe, but only for single works of art of value, such as a bronze statue or bust. For ordinary industrial purposes there is a simple process of casting in sand from wooden or metal patterns, patterns which effect an enormous saving of time and trouble, because the patterns, instead of being destroyed in such casting, can be used over and over again.

Shortly before I left the Madras School of Arts, I introduced the teaching of this method into the metal work class there. The subject was dropped afterwards, but I am glad to hear that Mr. Chatterton, who is now in charge of the School, has taken it up again. I must say that if District Boards and Municipalities would take up questions of this kind, and employ trained workmen to go round to the various industrial centres and give practical demonstrations of improved processes and apparatus, they might do much more than Schools of Art and Technical Institutes ever will be able to accomplish in spreading technical knowledge among the artisans of the country. I would commend this suggestion to the Committee of the Indian Industrial Association.

Before I have finished, I will allude briefly to Indian art industries, a subject which was discussed before you not so very long ago by Mr. S. J. Tellery. In some ways, art work must be treated quite differently to ordinary commercial productions, but there is one principle which is common to both—you must establish the home market on a healthy basis before you look abroad for foreign markets. We have heard a great deal lately of the decline of Indian art industries, but in nine out of ten of the proposals, which have been made for reviving them, this principle has been entirely disregarded. Both official and private exertions have been directed almost entirely towards the encouragement of the export trade. I must repeat again and again my strongest conviction that this is an entirely mistaken policy. First find out and remove, if you can, the causes which have led to the degradation of Indian Art in India, and the export trade will revive and expand almost automatically. On the other hand, unless effective measures are taken, before it is too late, to give back to Indian Art the prestige it has lost in India, and to remove those artificial impediments to its natural development which have existed so long, it needs no prophet to foresee that the export trade in Indian artware will die an unnatural death.

I have tried to explain in two papers, published in the *Calcutta Review*, my reasons for believing that the decay of Indian art is mostly due to the fatal mistake which has been made in Indian public buildings in supplanting the living traditional styles of Indian architecture by imitations of modern European scholastic styles. Architecture is the principal door through which the artistic sense of the people finds expression. If that door is mostly choked with rubbish, as it is in India, is it surprising that art industries should decline? I know that this theory is not easily grasped by those who imagine that art knowledge means only a knowledge of pictures, and that this knowledge can be acquired by going to exhibitions or by making a picture collection in the same way as collections of postage-stamps or bric-a-brac are made. If I wished to estimate the value of any one's pretensions to art knowledge, I would look first at his house, his tables and chairs, his carpets and everything connected with the routine of his home, last of all at his pictures; for, if he does not understand the elements of art, it is not likely that he will have a correct appreciation of higher and more abstruse principles. In England, there has been lately a remarkable art movement which is likely to have a most important influence on public opinion, since it has been strong enough to persuade that venerable, but somewhat effete institution, the Royal Academy, to modify some of its hoary traditions.

While England and Europe generally are beginning to free themselves from the corrupt artistic influences of the last two centuries, it is not encouraging to find that Indian art feeling is far more debased in the great centres of European civilisation than it is in remote towns and villages. But why, I will ask, do Indians wait for Government initiative in the matter? No one compels you to go on following what is now recognised as the depraved European taste of several generations ago, which unfortunately was imported into India long before Art Schools were established either in England or in India. You have magnificent examples of your own architecture and art to follow. Government would hail with the greatest satisfaction any efforts you made to rescue Indian art from the ruin which is overtaking it. Queen Victoria herself employed the Indian artisans whom India neglects, to decorate her Palace at Osborne in Indian style. Why then do the Princes, aristocracy and wealthy men of India continue to build those monstrous and ridiculous palaces and mansions, in imitation of the most corrupt period of European art, to the detriment of the art industries of the country, and to the disgust of every one whose artistic sense is in any degree developed?

II.

In the last edition of the "*Encyclopædia Britannica*" the writer of an article on Indian industries and trade makes a mis-statement which is very typical of the one-sided view often taken of Indian industrial problems. In the paragraph on textiles he gives the following information regarding this industry:—"Next after agriculture, the spinning and weaving of cotton at steam-mills is the most important industry in India." He proceeds to give the number of mills 186, looms 38,420, and persons employed 163,200. The output of yarn by these mills is given as 501,294,000 lbs. Of this total, according to the writer, 243,000,000 lbs. is exported, and apparently the mills themselves consume enough yarn to make up 95,320,000 lbs. of woven goods; there is, therefore, a balance of 162,974,000 lbs., of yarn turned out by the steam-mills, or nearly double the quantity consumed by themselves, which is unaccounted for either by exports or by manufactured cloth. Besides this surplus there is an import of cotton yarn to the value of 24,600,000 rupees. Where does all this yarn go to? If the writer had reflected on the significance of his own figures, he would have been reminded of the existence of a native hand-loom industry which numbers over one-third of the entire industrial population of India, or, roughly, about 5,000,000 workmen! He has fallen into the common, but very serious, mistake of taking the industries, mainly supported by European capital, to represent the whole industry of India; yet for every man employed by the European mills there are about thirty skilled weavers at the native hand-looms. The amount of yarn imported from Europe, added to that turned out by the Indian mills, is by no means a true index to the importance of this gigantic native industry, for in a great many districts the weavers use only hand-spun yarn which is made locally. I am not aware of any reliable statistics as to the value of the entire out-turn of the native hand-looms, but it must very largely exceed the whole production of the steam-mills. Without putting too much reliance on census statistics one can get some idea of the importance to India of this hand-loom industry by endeavouring to imagine what must be produced by the shuttles of an effective army of the most skilful weavers, approximating in number to the entire population of London, plied with the enduring patience of the Oriental through most of the hours of daylight, week in, week out. If it is a remarkable fact that they have been able to survive so long the competition of all the marvellous textile machinery of modern Europe, it is still more surprising that an authority on Indian affairs, writing for a great standard work of reference, should ignore altogether the part they take in the Indian industrial system.

The total number of the artisan population of India, actually engaged in industrial pursuits, is approximately twelve millions. Compared with European countries this may seem to bear a very small proportion to the total population, but it must be remembered that owing to climate, habits of life and social conditions, the wants of the natives of India are very small compared with what Europeans consider to be essential for their well-being. The native has few of the artificial requirements which inexorable custom imposes upon us, and even fewer of the luxuries for which we crave. The artisans of India are hereditary handicraftsmen, bound together by the laws of caste into compact and thoroughly disciplined organisations which had their exact counterpart in the old Trade Guilds of Europe. The European Guilds have ceased to exist, but the laws of heredity even now play a not inconsiderable part in European industry. The unrivalled skill of English potters, inherited from many generations of potter families, is one conspicuous instance, and many others might be cited. It is generally the case in India that this great industrial organisation is looked upon compassionately as an interesting relic of past ages, doomed to be dissolved before the irresistible march of modern scientific progress. But, surely, this is only the view of a sect of narrow-minded thinkers, ignorant of an important phase of modern European industrial development, who would date the beginning of the world from the invention of the first steam-engine and would consign to a general limbo of disuse everything of greater antiquity.

Is there sufficient warrant for the assumption that this great industrial machine is so hopelessly antiquated and impossible of development that it must be treated as of no account in India's commercial future? Are these twelve million skilled handicraftsmen inevitably doomed to degenerate into mill "hands," packed together in over-crowded cities as the brainless drudges of automatic machinery? Is there no hope that modern intelligence and modern science can find a way for making use of the vast industrial resources which have afforded India wealth and prosperity ever since the dawn of civilisation? The answers which Indian administrators give to these questions are of vital importance to the well-being of the country. Some years ago, in the course of official investigations into the condition of native art industries, I had special opportunities of studying the state of the native hand-loom industry. Those whose knowledge of Indian handicrafts is gathered only from curiosity shops and exhibitions may be led to believe that the native textile industry is mostly concerned in the manufacture of carpets and of the brocaded silks, cloths of gold and other gorgeous apparel, which there represent the work of Indian weavers. They will be surprised to learn that the manufacture of such *articles de luxe* occupies a small fraction only of the whole industry, and is of comparatively little commercial importance. By far the largest proportion of the weavers, scattered throughout the innumerable villages and towns of India, are occupied in making the common white and coloured cloths which are the only wear of the great mass of the population. That they have suffered enormously from European competition may be realised by the fact that the yearly imports of foreign piece-goods, according to the last returns, were valued at about eighteen million pounds sterling. Even in the by-gone days when Indian cotton goods were only prevented from overflowing European markets by high protective duties, Indian weavers have always been kept in a state of semi-slavery by the rapacity of the native middlemen. Now that the imports of European piece-goods have made the middlemen largely independent of the native weaver's labour, their condition is still more miserable. But their sedentary occupation renders them unfit for most kinds of manual labour, and until famine drives them out-of-doors, the weavers will cling to their looms. They are skilful workmen and patient, uncomplaining creatures, satisfied if by working most of daylight hours they can earn enough for bare subsistence. Mechanically, the ordinary native loom is very much the same as the old-fashioned European loom, still largely used in Scandinavia. In other industries modern inventions, such as the sewing machine, have been introduced into India, and readily adopted by native artisans; but, though this industry is of far greater importance than all the other native handicrafts, no one has ever tried to help the unfortunate weaver, and he is generally in too abject a condition to attempt to help himself.

The first and one of the most important improvements ever made in weaving apparatus was invented in 1733 by an English weaver, John Kay, who, wearied with the slow process of throwing the shuttle by hand, contrived a simple mechanical device for jerking the shuttle backwards and forwards by pulling a string attached to a lever. This not only relieved him of the labour of throwing the shuttle by hand, but doubled the speed of the shuttle! John Kay's invention, called the fly-shuttle, gave an enormous impetus to the English trade, and was the beginning of England's supremacy in the textile industry. In the course of one of my official tours I saw some European fly-shuttle looms in a Mission Industrial School in the Madras Presidency, and was much struck with the facility with which they were worked by native converts who had had no previous experience in weaving. But such is the helplessness and conservatism of the native caste-weaver that even when such an effective improvement is brought to his doors, he is very slow to adopt it, and I never came across it in any of the looms of the thousands of caste-weavers, which I visited in the Madras Presidency. However, several years afterwards, I was taking part in an enquiry into the industries of Bengal, and in an old official report I found an allusion to a large and unusually flourishing colony of weavers in Serampore, and the surrounding districts, whose prosperity was attributed to an improved loom in which the shuttle was jerked by a string attached to a lever. Serampore, which is situated on the Hooghly, a little above

Calcutta, was one of the settlements of the Danish East India Company, and among other interesting historical associations it is famous for having given shelter to William Carey when the old John Company found his presence in British territory inconvenient. It was from Carey's printing press at Serampore that the first vernacular translation of the Bible was issued, followed by many others. A visit to Serampore showed me that the improved loom, referred to in the report, was simply the adaptation of the fly-shuttle to the ordinary native loom. I further ascertained how it was that only in this quiet little corner of India the caste-weavers had been induced to adopt this most effective improvement. It appears that sixty or seventy years ago some Europeans had started a hand-loom factory and imported European looms. The local weavers were employed in the factory and had learnt the use of the fly-shuttle and a few simple labour-saving devices in the preparation of warp. The factory, however, did not exist for long, but when it was closed the weavers went back to their ordinary work, taking the fly-shuttle and other improvements with them. The effect of these has been just as remarkable in the case of the Serampore weavers as it was in the English hand-loom industry more than a century before. The hand-loom workers in the surrounding districts to the number of about 10,000, who adopted these improvements, have doubled their earnings, and though they are in close proximity to the great port of Calcutta, where day by day steamers unload their thousands of bales of foreign piece-goods, they have been able to maintain a fairly prosperous and independent condition in the face of the competition of the power-loom. The Bengal Government promptly took action to place the 400,000 weavers in other districts in a position to take advantage of these improvements by sending selected weavers from every district to be taught at Serampore. At the same time carpenters were sent to be taught to adapt the fly-shuttle to the native looms in the least expensive manner. The ordinary native loom can be converted into a fly-shuttle loom at a cost of about ten rupees. The question also began to arouse public interest, and some of the delegates of the National Congress were inspired to organise an Industrial Exhibition in Calcutta at the Congress Meeting in 1901, where the practical working of the fly-shuttle was demonstrated side by side with the old native loom, and a number of caste weavers were brought to see it. The Exhibition is apparently to be a permanent side-show to the political gathering of the Congress, for another was held in Bombay last December and seems to have aroused the sympathy of the

Government, who doubtless recognise that it will be an unmixed blessing to India if the Congress party temper the fervour of their political propaganda with rather more practical interest in the industrial development of the country. The Indian Press aided me in making the facts known in other parts of India, with the result that during the last twelve months the question has been taken up more or less vigorously in almost every province of British India and in many of the Native States, especially in Mysore, where four weaving schools have been sanctioned expressly for teaching weavers the use of the fly-shuttle. In the Bombay Presidency, energetic steps have been taken by District Boards and by local officials interested in helping the hand-loom industry. Grants-in-aid amounting to 50,000 rupees have been voted and schools have been opened at Sholapur, Bijapur and other great weaving centres. A recent report sent in to the District Board of Bijapur states that the school has created the greatest interest among the neighbouring weavers, numbering about 12,000, who are coming in every day from the surrounding villages to receive instruction.

While it is yet far too soon to expect actual results which can demonstrate statistically the benefits gained by the weavers from these new centres of instruction, it is quite possible to establish from facts already known a sound policy for the future official attitude towards the great hereditary handicrafts of India. It is already a fact beyond dispute that two or three simple mechanical improvements have enabled about 10,000 weavers in the districts round Serampore to nearly double their earnings—that is, instead of an average of 4 or 5 rupees monthly, they now earn from 7 to 9 rupees. There are various technical difficulties which prevent the fly-shuttle being used for all classes of weaving, but for the great majority of the weavers it would be an enormous advantage. Supposing that 4,000,000 weavers were thereby enabled to increase their earning in the same way as the Serampore weavers have done, it would mean that their total monthly earnings would be increased by 12,000,000 to 16,000,000 rupees, or an annual increase of 144,000,000 to 192,000,000 rupees, a sum approximating to two-thirds of the total value of the yearly imports of foreign piece-goods. When it is further considered that the improvements which have already done so much for the Serampore weavers are the very first of a long series begun in 1733, and that the latest English hand-loom is five or six times as effective as the old-fashioned loom, now used at Serampore, it is possible to realise the splendid future which might be opened out for the Indian hand-loom industry. There can hardly be a doubt that were the most effective modern hand-looms placed in the hands of the skilled and industrious Indian weavers, they could supply the greater part of the textile requirements of India at prices with which the highly capitalised power-loom factories would be unable to compete. On the other hand, the spinning mills of India would benefit very largely by the increased demand for yarn which a prosperous hand-loom industry would create.

I had an opportunity recently of seeing a demonstration of the capabilities of the latest English hand-loom in a factory at Cairo. A Belgian Company had imported the looms which, though a marvel of mechanical ingenuity, are perfectly simple in manipulation. Under the supervision of a single trained foreman a number of Arab boys and men, who had had no previous experience of weaving and were delighted at the opportunity of displaying their newly-acquired skill, were working these looms with a facility which was evidently a source of great satisfaction and profit both to themselves and to the Company. The results of the first year's working had been so satisfactory that the Company has resolved to extend its operations by a large increase of capital. It is already well known to the textile trade that of late years the hand-loom, under favourable conditions and in certain classes of weaving, has even in Europe been steadly regaining some of the ground which, it was believed, had been finally occupied by the power-loom. But I believe it has not yet been realised what a splendid field might be opened for it in countries like India and Egypt, where the old hand-loom industry is still alive and where the cost of skilled labour is very much less than it is in Europe. In Egypt, there are still 30,000 hand-loom weavers who, with the primitive hand-loom of antiquity, have yet survived the competition of the power-loom.

The existence of these great organised armies of skilled handicraftsmen, both in India and in Egypt, points to the unwisdom of working exclusively on the lines of Europe's nineteenth-century industrial methods in the economic development of these countries. If the village handicrafts of India can be developed to a high degree of prosperity by other methods surely it is nothing less than a crime to allow the villages to be depopulated and to crowd the inhabitants into filthy factories, polluting both earth and sky, where all their mental and moral faculties are debased. Should not the social evils caused by industrial development in Europe and America make Indian statesmen pause before they commit themselves to a policy which, if attended by many evils in Europe, would be a far greater curse to India? Hitherto, the view of India's industrial interests generally taken by Indian Administration has been that which Mr. Carnegie has deprecated. They have devoted the whole force of the State machinery to the development of the export trade, leaving the home industries to take care of themselves. They have nearly always assumed that India's industrial future is safe in the keeping of the enterprising and clear-headed merchants who control the trade of the great Indian sea-ports. But it must be clear that the interests of the capitalists engaged in Indian commercial enterprises run in a narrow groove and do not always coincide with the larger interests of the Empire. Already in Europe there are signs which indicate that before many generations have passed we shall come to regard many phases of the last century's industrial development as a hideous social nightmare. When electricity has taken the place it will eventually take in our industrial system, there can hardly be a doubt that many industries will return to the villages and many pestiferous rookeries in the great towns will be cleared off the face of the earth. Why then regard as the only policy in India that which means the multiplication of such social plague spots? India is intended both by

Nature and by the genius of her inhabitants to be a hand-worker's paradise. Why should we only employ methods originating in totally different conditions of social economy, and give her an inferno for her paradise ?—[*East and West, September, 1903.*]

III.

In the beginning of 1901, when I laid down the proposition that the soundest basis for the industrial regeneration of India was to be found in the revival of the great hand-loom industry, I was preaching a new and strange doctrine opposed to all accepted theories. The Government Commissions and Committees which, during many years, had attempted to deal with the problem, had always accepted the common theory, still maintained with some insistence but with considerably diminished authority, that skill in hand-weaving was a factor reduced to insignificance by modern mechanical invention and modern industrial methods. Official statistics of trade and industry at that time completely ignored the existence of hand-loom weaving as an industrial asset worth consideration, and that great storehouse of concentrated wisdom, the Encyclopædia Britannica, still records the then official view that India's greatest industry after agriculture is the manufacture of textile materials and fabrics carried on in Anglo-Indian power-loom mills.

Up to a few years ago, all the schemes which have been the outcome of twenty years' discussion of a subject which is even now only vaguely understood in India—technical education—have been based on the same fallacy. I believe it will be within the mark to state that in 1887, out of hundreds of so-called "Technical Institutes" opened with much enthusiasm and in many cases with a liberal grant of Government funds, not one per cent. took into account the existence of the hand-loom industry or the immense potentialities represented by it. India is fortunate if the great sums of money wasted on these technical schemes, the futility of which I pointed out at the time of their inception, are the last which will be thrown away on ill-conceived projects of the same kind.

The facts and inferences on which I ventured to propose an entirely new departure in principle and in practice were based partly on experience gained by me as Reporter on Arts and Industries to the Government of Madras, and partly on information dug out of old official records in Bengal. They were embodied in a paper read before the Indian Industrial Association of Calcutta, in July 1901. The lecture was reported in full by the Anglo-Indian and vernacular newspapers throughout India, and it induced hundreds of people in all parts of the country to begin practical investigations on the lines I advocated. The Press on this occasion asserted its great value as an educational agency, for no official, working only through official channels, would have the remotest chance of seeing his ideas taken up and worked into practical shape with the same speed as the co-operation of the Public Press has given to the movement for the revival of hand-loom weaving in India during the last six years. Hand-loom weaving has by this means been dragged from its obscurity and is not likely to be altogether passed over in any future discussions of industrial development in India.

The chief points with which I enforced my argument were, first, the remarkable revival of hand-loom weaving in some European countries, and, second, the hitherto unnoticed existence of many thousands of weavers in the districts adjoining Serampore, near Calcutta, who by adopting the old-fashioned English fly-shuttle loom, and a few simple but very practical improvements in the preparatory processes of weaving, had raised themselves into a comparatively flourishing and independent position, a striking contrast to that of their fellow-workers in other less advanced districts. This fact had, indeed, attracted the attention of a Bengal Civilian who had been deputed by Government, eleven years before, to advise upon industrial education, but he, having no technical knowledge of industrial processes, failed to realise the significance of the fact, and no official action was taken upon it. Even now, after six years' discussion and practical experiment, I do not believe there exists in India a more useful object-lesson for those who are endeavouring to ameliorate the condition of the hand-loom weaver.

Among the first to start practical work on the lines of my proposals was the late Mr. P. C. Ghosh, who, as Editor of the "Indian Mechanic," had been an earnest advocate of *Swadeshi* principles long before *Swadeshi* became a political battle-cry. He commenced the manufacture of improved looms and apparatus on the Serampore model in his workshops at Hooghly, and at the first Industrial Exhibition of 1901, held under the auspices of the Congress at Calcutta, he gave a practical demonstration of them, side by side with the old native loom. He also distributed ten thousand copies of my lecture which he had reprinted at his own expense. In 1902, he was invited to the Bombay Presidency to give instruction in the Serampore processes to the large colonies of weavers in Sholapur and its neighbourhood. There, unfortunately, soon after he had started work with a great promise of success, he fell a victim to plague—and India lost in him a very zealous and able worker in the cause of industrial progress.

This valuable work has, however, been continued by his partner and successor, Mr. P. C. Dey of Chinsurah, who has supplied models of the Serampore apparatus to almost every part of India, besides teaching the use of it for a very moderate charge to numbers of weavers and others who have been sent to him, and giving practical demonstrations at a great many *melas* and Exhibitions. Since 1901, Mr. Dey has sent out nearly 800 complete looms and about 1,400 "lays" or the essential working part of the fly-shuttle loom. This means that he has been instrumental in starting about 2,200 fly-shuttle looms in many different centres throughout India. Probably no one has done more practical work than this in helping the hand-loom industry.

The Bengal Government in 1901, translated my lecture into four vernaculars for distribution to the District Boards. Direct support on the part of Government in Bengal has been limited so far to a grant of a few hundred rupees given by Sir John Woodburn in 1901-2, to enable a few weavers to undergo a month's training under my supervision at Serampore. The hesitation of the Government of India to commit itself to a change of the view maintained by its advisers for so many years has no doubt prevented many of the Local Governments from giving a more active support to a movement which has gained so much impetus from non-official agencies. Sir George Watt, formerly Reporter on Economic Products to the Government of India, declared about four years ago that the extinction of hand-loom weaving in India was inevitable, and that "to bolster up the effete methods and appliances of bygone times would of necessity involve the suppression of national progress." Lord Curzon at the Delhi Durbar repeated the old argument that the hand-loom must inevitably give way to the power-loom "just as the hand punkah is being superseded by the electric fan," but in 1905, he was sufficiently impressed by the arguments on the other side to sanction a comprehensive scheme I drew up for developing hand-loom weaving in Bengal. This scheme, however, has not yet been put into operation.

Many of the Native States have, from the first, given a vigorous support to the movement. I believe Mysore led the way by opening a number of schools and experimental workshops. Travancore followed, and the Baroda State, with the keen personal interest of the Gaekwar and of the Revenue Minister, Mr. R. C. Dutt, has for some years taken a leading part in investigating all the practical problems connected with the question. Recently, the Madras Government has joined in with a strong official support. Mr. Alfred Chatterton who in 1901, after consultation with me, began a series of experiments for his own information in the Madras School of Arts, for some years maintained an ambiguous attitude on the whole question, but he has now become an active worker in the cause of hand-loom weaving, and after further personal investigation in Bengal he has lately induced his Government to establish a number of hand-loom factories in various great weaving centres in the Southern Presidency. It seems like a return to old John Company days to find an Indian Government engaged directly in the weaving trade, and as private enterprise in the last two years has shown itself quite ready and able to establish hand-weaving factories without Government assistance, it is difficult to see the advantage of official weaving establishments conducted on commercial principles, when, as Mr. Chatterton has admitted, they stand in need of expert advice and provoke more hostility and suspicion on the part of the local weavers than private undertakings of the same kind.

In fact, the real strength of the movement and the most hopeful sign for its future progress are shown in the eagerness and capacity with which non-official Indians have thrown themselves into it. I have myself, since 1901, carried on a voluminous correspondence with Indians all over the country anxious for advice and information, and the growing confidence in the prospects of hand-loom weaving as a profitable undertaking for small capitalists has led to the opening of not a few hand-loom factories under entirely Indian management. The yearly exhibitions and demonstrations of hand-loom apparatus which is now the most prominent feature of the industrial programme of the Congress have been most helpful in this direction. In the first Exhibition of 1901-02, organised by Mr. J. Chaudhry, the late Mr. P. C. Ghose was the sole exhibitor, but in 1906-07, when the Congress again met in Calcutta, there were besides Messrs. Hattersley of Keighley, who on my recommendation sent a special representative to demonstrate the latest English hand-weaving appliances, adapted for Indian requirements, about thirty Indian exhibitors from different parts of the country, some of them showing improvements of their own invention.

It does not, however, promote confidence in the wisdom of political intrusions into the field of industrial economics to find that Bengal, one of the most promising fields in all India for hand-loom factories, has been the one province which has been induced by *Swadeshi* politicians to adopt the very *un-Swadeshi* system of power-loom mills, a policy which, carried to its logical conclusion, must severely cripple any project for raising the unfortunate village weaver from his present state of helplessness and ignorance. It is true that the boycott of foreign manufactures, which is part of the Swadeshi programme in Bengal, has for the time being given so much remunerative work to the village weavers that the number of working hand-loom weavers in the province has, it is said, been doubled; but a scheme based only on political passion and without any sound economic or educational basis is not likely to give the industry anything but temporary relief.

This confusion of ideas, natural, perhaps, in the great multitude of counsellors which has now entered the field, seems to make it desirable to restate some of the economic, ethical and artistic principles involved in the whole question. When six years ago I expressed my conviction that Indian weavers, with proper appliances and instruction, could produce profitably a great part, if not all, of the textiles now imported from Europe, the possibility of increasing the wealth of the country by some twenty million pounds sterling a year was to me a question of far less interest than the means by which that result might be achieved. The possibility of building up on the foundation of the old Indian village community and of the Indian hereditary handicraft system a strong self-reliant, intelligent, co-operative organisation adapted to the present and future needs of the country, yet avoiding the terrible evils which modern science has brought into the industrial system of Europe, seems to me always a matter of infinitely greater importance to India than the prospective material gain, however great that might be. As to the question whether the power-loom will or will not supersede the hand-loom, the answer is simple. As long as the artistic sense is part of the intellectual equipment of humanity, so long will hand-labour be as necessary in weaving as it is in any other art; and thus so far as art is involved in weaving, the hand-loom will never be superseded. When weaving is reduced to a purely automatic movement of a shuttle, the power-loom will supersede the hand-loom whenever the cost of power is less than the cost of hand-labour. Mr. Chatterton, in a recent lecture, stated that wherever the hand-loom still exists in Europe, there are special reasons for its survival which are not applicable to India. This is an entire misapprehension of the case. The two reasons, artistic and economical, apply with exactly the same force in India and in Europe. The hand-loom exists in Europe wherever one or other of two conditions prevail. The first is when hand-labour is cheaper than the cost of mechanical power; the second is when public taste is sufficiently developed to discriminate between the real art of the hand-worker and the sham art of the automatic machine. In the last fifty years, in Europe, there has been a great advance in artistic knowledge and education, accompanied by an improvement in public taste, and a corresponding revival of hand-loom weaving. In India, there has been during the last hundred years a continuous decline of public taste, so that at the present time the educated Indians probably stand behind the rest of the civilised world in artistic understanding. There has been a complete neglect of art education and a corresponding decline in the higher branches of weaving, and many of the most beautiful fabrics for which India has been famous from time immemorial are no longer produced, because they have ceased to be appreciated. On the purely industrial side, hand-loom weaving has declined in India only because the whole question of technical education as applied to Indian handicrafts has been as much neglected as art education. Even now, though the commercial interests of hand-loom weaving are only second in importance to those of agriculture, there is not yet in Government service anywhere in India a single expert in weaving, as expert knowledge is understood in Europe. The result is that technical questions which were common knowledge in Europe a century ago are still left to be worked out again in India by costly and tedious experiments conducted by engineers, agriculturists, or chemists whose knowledge of weaving is necessarily limited to the scope of their individual experiments. Hand-labour for weaving in India is never really more expensive than mechanical power and is not likely to be so for many generations. The Indian handicraftsmen are only being beaten by the power-loom, because, in the first place, the artistic understanding of the people has degenerated, and, in the second place, because the weavers themselves are totally ignorant of the improvements in hand processes and hand-apparatus which have been made in the last 150 years in Europe.

Though I have discriminated between art and industry in weaving, it is an exceedingly difficult matter to fix any dividing line between them. It may be stated generally that the higher the artistic sense is developed, the less distinguishable is the difference between the two. Even in plain weaving by hand processes there are beauties patent to the educated eye which mechanical processes can hardly obtain. But what I want chiefly to emphasise is that a national decline in artistic taste spells not only intellectual impoverishment but commercial disaster, and for this reason the problem of the industrial reorganisation of India is as much an artistic as an economic one. It is certainly not from sentimental or purely artistic reasons that England since 1857 has spent millions of hard cash on schools of art and design, but because the Government after many years was forced to the conclusion that other countries with better artistic knowledge, were driving many English manufactures out of the market. It is also certain that India's ruinous loss in industrial capacity would have been far less serious, or have been avoided entirely, if during the last hundred years a sound artistic policy had been established. At the present time we seem to be as far off as ever from the realisation of those measures which are necessary to prevent further deterioration in that great commercial asset represented by India's artistic power and understanding. India has had no share in the marked artistic revival which has been progressing in Europe for the last fifty years, though her traditional art knowledge is being continually exploited in every direction for the benefit of European art and manufacture.

Unless we take for granted that Indian art must necessarily, in the name of scientific progress, be dragged through the same mire as that in which art in Europe began to wallow more than a century ago, the theory that the hand-loom is doomed to disappear is wholly untenable on artistic grounds. Let us now begin to consider from an ethical standpoint the merits of the present European system which the advocates of "progress" wish to substitute for Indian hand-loom weaving. The only ideal the power-loom factory has in view is cheapness for the purchaser. But at what a frightful sacrifice of the miserable humanity which is dragged behind the car of progress is this cheapness obtained! Mr. Allen Clarke, one of the best authorities on the subject—for he was the son of a mill-hand and himself one of them—has described it graphically in his book on "The Effects of the Factory System." "It is marvellous," he says, "that any good is still left in the mill-hands of Lancashire. They are slaves of the machines, instead of the machines being the slaves of men." The system is, he declares, unhealthy, dangerous, bad for mind and body, injurious in its effects in family life, unfitting women for motherhood, cursing the children and causing the people to deteriorate. It is probably true that in the majority of Indian mills the physical welfare of the worker is better provided for than in Europe, and perhaps on this account Sir George Watt says that the objections to the system are "misguided and sentimental." On the other hand a Parsi mill-owner recently described the conditions of labour in the Bombay mills as revealing "a degrading and disgraceful spectacle of cold-blooded inhumanity." This is synchronous not with a period of bad trade, but with an unusual burst of prosperity due to the *Swadeshi* movement.

It may be that legislation, by imposing restrictions on the hours of labour and improving sanitary conditions, may check the rapacity of mill-owners and shareholders, and it may be that the latter in their own interests will some day do as much for their employees as wise and considerate men do for their horses and cattle, but even the wisest and most humane cannot in the pursuit of the ideal of cheapness make the modern system of labour, in power-loom mills, otherwise than intellectually and morally degrading. Nor can they remove the even greater evils which the system brings with it—the over-crowded, filthy, air-polluted cities, the depopulation of rural districts and the struggles between capital and labour which in Western countries constantly threaten the very foundations of society.

When one observes the effect upon social life in Europe and America of the system of industrial organisation created by the application of mechanical power, it is surely reasonable to pause and ask whether it is so inevitable that India should abandon entirely her old industrial methods and follow in the wake of what is called progress in Europe. The Indian weaver has now no choice between the servitude of the power-loom mill and the servitude of the village sowcar. But is this the last word of science and of statecraft? It would be foolish and wicked to suppose so; and herein lies the fallacy of the argument that India must necessarily sacrifice all its old industrial methods because Europe did so fifty or a hundred years ago. The present European industrial system, with all its obvious defects, was founded on the first clumsy and crude experiments of modern mechanical science commenced little more than a century ago. The scientific improvements of to-day are thrown in the scrap-heap to-morrow. Is India, then, blindly to take this clumsy, cruel and immature system as a model to imitate, or should she not rather, instead of rejecting as useless the institutions on which her whole industrial organisation has been based, try to develop them as far as present means allow, with an intelligent preparation for what the science of the future will surely bring?

Mr. Chatterton, in a lecture before the Southern Indian Association, recently declared that much false sentiment has been wasted on the village weaver. It is common for modern scientists to profess a fine contempt for sentiment. Sentiment, they argue, did not help the hand-weavers of Europe nor will it in the long run save the hand-weavers of India. The village weaving industry represents thousands of generations of India's artistic culture. This culture, however, according to the scientist's argument, is only a matter of sentiment which we practical men of the present day neither feel nor want. Therefore let the village industry go, if only we can devise some means for cheap manufactures sufficient for India's present needs. Sentiment, nevertheless, is a force more powerful than scientists are generally willing to allow. It is sentiment which makes the weaver cling to his village life instead of clamouring for employment in the Bombay mills. This same sentiment has, therefore, helped to save for India an industry worth commercially more than the whole of the Anglo-Indian industries. Sentiment, or the artistic sense, is even now in Europe bringing about a revolt against the rabid commercialism of the last century, and sentiment will sooner or later be served by a high and better science than what we call science to-day. There is as much false science as there is false sentiment. Europe has now realised from the experience of the last two centuries that there is a science in art. The destruction of Indian Art which is going on under British rule is a loss to civilisation and to humanity which can and should be avoided, if Indian industrial reformers will bring to their work the true science which Europe has painfully learnt only after the destruction of all her traditional art. It should not now he necessary for India to follow the bull-in-the-china-shop methods which we have too often applied in the name of European civilisation, science and progress.

It is a comparatively easy matter to bring into India the practical knowledge for manufacturing all the textiles required in the country. But to attain that object without sacrificing all the present village industry and the traditional art which it represents, is a problem of far greater difficulty, requiring not only scientific and artistic knowledge, but statesmanship, tact, patience and perseverance. The first step to be taken is undoubtedly to release the village weaver from the clutches of the money-lender and make him a free man. Industrial progress is impossible when the weavers are in their present state of servitude. A few years ago I drew attention in the Press to an admirable scheme started by Mr. A. F. Maconochie, I. C. S., while Collector of Sholapur, a great weaving centre in the Bombay Presidency; the ordinary hand-loom weaver in India gets his yarn and other materials from the village banker on credit, and sells the finished products on terms fixed by the banker, who generally takes cruel advantage of the necessities of the weaver. Mr. Maconochie's scheme is practically a Co-operative Bank which purchases yarn, etc, at wholesale rates and retails it on credit to the weavers at a small profit. It also advances cash to help the weavers over the slack season, taking the finished cloths as pledges to be redeemed when the marriage season makes a brisk demand for them. In this way the weavers get their raw materials at reasonable rates and obtain the best market price for their labour. The scheme, originally started for charitable relief after the famine of 1899, has been placed on a regular business footing since 1901. In 1904, Mr. T. J. Pitre, the officer in charge of it, reported that out of 300 weavers on his books at least 25 had paid off their old debts and recovered their mortgaged property from the sowcars. The weavers were so punctual in the repayment of advances that the law had not been invoked in a single instance, and while their condition had greatly improved, the scheme itself was a fair financial success.

It ought not be impossible by the cordial co-operation of Government and people to spread such an excellent and practical system throughout the country and thus release the weaver from the crushing burden of debt which famine and times of scarcity constantly impose upon him. When he is a free man he will not be found quite so stupid or so unteachable as popular opinion represents him. He has at any rate great hereditary skill which is recognised even in Europe as a very important qualification. Mr. Chatterton complains that he objects to turning out more yards of cloth than he has been accustomed to. But the objection is perfectly natural and sensible as long as the only result of increased production is to put more money into the hands of his task-master, the Sowcar.

When the weaver has been released from this tyranny, he will be able to take full advantage of such opportunities for using modern labour-saving appliances as may be afforded him. It should be the duty of every District Board and Municipality throughout India to provide such opportunities, but sympathetic personal interest on the part of zemindars and great landholders is more likely to be fruitful than the ordinary perfunctory measures of these bodies. The Mysore Government has recently followed Mr. Maconochie's excellent example by authorising the formation of a Weaver's Co-operative Society in Bangalore and by advancing it money up to Rs. 2,000 free of interest. It has also undertaken to supply models of improved looms and appliances free of cost for the purpose of experiment by members and ordered suitable facilities to be provided for elementary instruction of weavers' children in day and night schools in the city. All these measures are entirely in the right direction and part of the same enlightened policy in art and industrial matters which has distinguished the Government of Mysore in recent years.

Hand-loom factories may undoubtedly be very useful agencies for spreading the knowledge of improved methods and appliances all over the country, but they must by no means be regarded as an entirely satisfactory substitute for the existing industrial organisation or as the only means of saving the latter from annihilation. In the first place, they will be directed mostly by small capitalists without the slightest artistic knowledge or tradition, and without any other ideal except cheapness of production. Their educational use will be comparatively restricted because the weavers employed in them will be nearly all drawn from the classes lowest in skill and intelligence, which will usually prefer to remain in a dependent position rather than make use of their training as a means of gaining an independent livelihood for themselves. And unless, as I have said before, the weaver is freed from the hands of the Sowcars, he will have no incentive for attempting to better his position. That this will be the case is shown by the fact that the Basel Mission hand-weaving factories on the Malabar Coast although they have been working with great financial success for many years, have had practically no educational influence on the weavers in the surrounding districts. Hand-weaving factories under Government control, like those started by Mr. Chatterton, may be more successful in this way if artistic supervision is adequately provided for, if commerical aims are subordinated to the educational, and if the not unnatural suspicions of the weavers can be overcome by tact and patience. It is not surprising that these ignorant, long-suffering folk, who have endured so much in the last century, should be rather sceptical of the benevolent intentions suddenly manifested on their behalf by the paternal Government. Well-conducted factories might indeed be extremely useful as educational institutions if the better class of weavers could be induced to serve in them, not as permanent workers, but for a fixed period, on the understanding that when their time had expired they would receive as part payment for their labour a gift of the improved apparatus they had been trained to use.

It is a remarkable circumstance that the great number of weavers in the neighbourhood of Serampore, estimated at about 10,000, who have doubled their earnings by the use of improved apparatus and processes, are said to have been indebted for this great gain to a hand-loom factory established at Serampore when that place was under Danish Government about eighty years ago. If the story be true, it is most instructive to note the difference between the success of this factory in its educational effect, and the failure of the German Mission weaving factories to influence the weavers in that neighbourhood. I cannot believe that this difference is entirely a matter of chance.

Denmark in the development of its agricultural industries on co-operative principles, has created a model for the rest of Europe. A great deal of attention is also paid to hand-weaving throughout Scandinavia. It is extremely probable, therefore, that in the administration of its Indian possessions the Danish Government made an organised effort to develop an industry so closely connected with agriculture as hand-loom weaving is in India, and I have little doubt that an investigation into the old Danish records of Serampore would prove this to be the case. The process and appliances used are so admirably adapted to the needs of the Indian industry that it is difficult, even with the great advance in hand-weaving appliances made in recent years, to suggest improvements likely to be adopted by ordinary weavers. It cannot be repeated too often that by the use of the Serampore processes (which involve no departure from the present organisation of the hand-weaving industry) in conjunction with appliances which can be adapted to the ordinary village loom at a capital cost of about fifteen rupees, the hand weaver of plain or simply-patterned cloth can double his present earnings.

Another point to be noted is that whereas mechanical improvements in hand-looms, such as the fly-shuttle, have a somewhat restricted application, some of the Serampore improvements in the preparatory processes and appliances, used before the warp is ready for the loom, are applicable to every kind of weaving throughout India. The most important is a simple apparatus for winding threads which costs only two or three rupees and reduces the labour of winding to at least a twentieth part of the old Indian system. The practical value of this, which is often overlooked in the keen discussion of the rival merits of improved hand-looms, can be best realised when it is known that in the ordinary Indian method of weaving plain cotton cloth, half the cost of the finished cloth is incurred before the thread is put on the loom for weaving. Moreover, without these preliminary improvements the advantage of using better looms is very often nullified.

The appliances now in use in Serampore and the surrounding districts are practically the same as those with which the English hand-weavers at the close of the eighteenth century trebled their earnings and turned the tables against their Indian competitors. Their adaptability to Indian conditions has been amply proved, and there is not the slightest doubt that the position of the hand-loom industry would be immensely strengthened if the weavers throughout India could be placed in a position to follow the example of their Serampore brethren.

The measures proposed by Mr. Chatterton for achieving this end differ essentially from the original example. He regards the present organisation of the weaving industry as hopeless, and by leaving the village weavers severely alone he would force them, when at last driven to extremities, to enter his model weaving factories. He would thus sweep away entirely all the artistic traditions of the famous Indian industry and reduce the weavers to the condition of day labourers under the control of individual capitalists who have no other qualifications than their knowledge of up-to-date mechanical appliances, and no other ideal than that of filling their own pockets. This is an easy policy to follow, but I fear it has very little else to recommend it.

It is easier to take the line of least resistance, and bend or break everything Indian into a European mould, than it is to promote a new life in Indian institutions by adapting them to their modern environment. It is easier to dissolve the old Indian village communities than to make them an integral part of the administrative system. It is easier to fabricate sham Classic and Gothic architecture for public buildings than to acquire the knowledge and artistic skill necessary for adapting the living traditions of Indian architecture to present-day administrative uses. It is easier to foist a travesty of Western culture upon India than to revive the old spirit in her ancient institutions. And it is certainly easier to leave the old Indian industrial system alone than to restore its vitality and help it to combat on fair terms the influences which are now destroying it.

The Serampore example points a better way than the one which Mr. Chatterton would take. Instead of degrading the Indian weaver into a factory hand, I would take the co-operative system practised with such signal success in Denmark as a model easily adaptable to the Indian weaving industry, and an ideal both economically and artistically sound. There is nothing in the most scientific modern process of weaving which could not be adapted to this system whenever it can be usefully employed, and the principle of division of labour which it implies is already recognised to a much larger extent in the Indian industry than is commonly assumed. Some time ago, the writer of several articles in the London *Times*, on the causes of India's poverty, described the Indian weaving industry as being organised on the primitive system by which every village produced the cloth required by itself, and quoted Adam Smith to show the economic unsoundness of the principle. This description is only true as regards the manufacture of some of the coarsest descriptions of cloth used by villagers, and is by no means applicable to the industry as a whole. The weavers, as a rule, are organised into industrial communities, sometimes numbering thousands of workers, who either through middlemen or by arrangements made by themselves, supply the requirements of large districts and even those of distant provinces. Formerly, as is well known, they were the centres of a great export trade also. The sudden cessation of this trade by the East India Company in the early part of the nineteenth century was probably the chief cause of the Indian weaver being now a helpless tool in the hands of the money-lender, and always the first victim in times of famine.

The principle of the Danish co-operative system as applied to dairy farming is the combination of a number of small proprietors for sending their products to a central factory in which each of them has a share proportionate to the quantity of his contributions. In the management of the factory each member has an absolutely equal voice, irrespective of his holding. Adapting such a system to the Indian weaving industry, each weaving community would have a central establishment under its own control which would arrange the purchase of materials at wholesale rates, prepare warps for the weavers' looms and organise the sale of the finished products. The actual weaving would be carried on as at present in the weavers' houses by the master weavers and their apprentices. A system of this kind would retain the economic advantages of the factory system and eliminate its many evils: it is obvious that a factory owned and controlled by the weavers themselves and worked only for their advantage is a very different thing to a factory controlled by capitalists, only for the purpose of exploiting the labour of their employees.

Neither would such a system prevent the weavers from making use of mechanical power to the fullest extent possible whenever they should find it advantageous to do so. But it would ensure that they always remained the masters of the machine instead of being its slaves, and this alone would tend to diminish the abuse of mechanical power in art industry. The present monstrous overgrowth of the factory system by which thousands of looms are crowded together under one roof originated from the impossibility, in the early days of the application of steam power to manufacturing purposes, of transmitting power over any considerable distances. Electricity and improvements in mechanical apparatus have changed all that and it would now be quite feasible, in Mysore for instance, to transmit the power from the Cauvery Falls to a vast number of weaving communities organised, as I have proposed, so that by turning a switch any weaver could convert his hand-loom into a power-loom whenever and for as long as he might choose. Modern science is also giving to the individual workman a means of freeing himself from the serfdom of the factory system by constantly lowering the minimum of power which can be profitably employed for industrial purposes. This means that many industries can be profitably worked on a much smaller scale than formerly.

It would not be at all surprising if the further advance in this direction which is inevitable should lead to a great revival of the old system of the single workshop with its master workman and apprentices. As I pointed out in a note on hand-loom weaving which was communicated to the Industrial Conference at Benares in 1905, the weaver's loom is a one-man power machine, and no advantage can be gained by applying more than a one-man power to it. As soon as the means of producing mechanical power and the application of it to industrial purposes is so far improved that the master workman and his five or six apprentices can use it at almost as cheap a rate as the employer of thousands of mill hands, the capitalist will find the field for the exploitation of skilled labour considerably restricted. The scientific principle of art industry will then once more assert itself.

Nothing is more remarkable in recent industrial developments in Europe and America than the re-introduction of methods and systems which, half a century ago, were ridiculed as effete and obsolete. The *Indian Trade Journal* recently stated the fact that the Japanese Government, in preparing to compete with European nations for commercial supremacy, " is showing a distinct reversion to former ways and methods." It especially drew attention to the steps which are being taken in Japan to reorganise the old Trade Guilds. The Journal summed up its comments in the following words:—" In re-adapting ancient methods Japan places herself somewhat in advance of other nations, the present national tendency being to stimulate and encourage trade by every possible means. Germany is perhaps the most advanced exponent of co-operative export trading, supported by the encouragement and aid of the State, and Japan does but go one step further in the same path. The lessons to be drawn from these considerations is that as the various Guilds grow in power and influence they will be able to dictate to European or American traders, unless the latter also enter into combination. This conclusion not only applies to trade in Japan, but also to trade in China, Manchuria and Korea."

In India, up to the present time, it has been usual to regard the caste system, which is the Indian counterpart of the Trade Guilds of Japan and Europe, as an impediment to economic progress, instead of the strongest basis for re-construction. As India in relation to art and industry always lags fifty years behind the least progressive thought of Europe, it is to be feared that bull-in-the-china-shop methods will continue to play havoc with Indian industrial institution for an indefinite period. Fifty years hence, perhaps, India will begin to discover that by following in the wake of European progress, instead of showing the way, she has thrown away a great deal of her most valuable possessions and reaped a crop of difficulties even more formidable than those she has to deal with now.—*East and West, August* 1907.

ART AND EDUCATION IN INDIA.

One of the greatest of Greek philosophers in a few memorable sentences has indicated the proper place of art in an ideal educational system:

> To use the beauties of earth as steps along which he mounts upwards, going from one to two, and from two to all fair forms, and from fair forms to fair actions, and from fair actions to fair notions, until from fair notions he arrives at the notion of absolute beauty, and at last knows what the essence of beauty is.

The Greeks, whose religious and philosophical ideas were founded on the closest observation of Nature, were deeply impressed by the invariable correlation between perfect beauty and perfect fitness, which is found in all of Nature's handiwork. The study of this universal law led them to regard the æsthetic faculty as part of that divine nature which lifts mankind above the brute creation, and must be cherished as the most precious endowment. Art, or the science of the beautiful, was to them a second religion; it became the daily bread of their intellectual life. To respect art was a national as well as an individual duty, because its influence tends to develop the best moral virtues in a citizen. It teaches patience and honesty, for no good art is produced without them. It teaches reverence, for admiration of the beautiful is the mainspring of the æsthetic faculty. It begets unselfishness, for æsthetic enjoyment is not obtained, like so many other of men's pleasures, at other people's expense, and it is increased when others share in it. It tends to elevate the mind and to create a dislike for all that is mean, dirty, and sordid.

English higher education in the nineteenth century was based theoretically on Greek traditions. But if one seeks in the national life for the effect of so-called classic education the difference between theory and practice can be seen too plainly. If the poetical inspiration of Shakespeare and Milton is often a hidden mystery to the Indian student who knows all his text and notes by heart, just as often the English schoolboy, who pores over his Greek idioms and syntax, remains in sublime ignorance of the ideas and impulses which brought the Greek nation to the highest summit of civilisation. The classic ideal in the modern English educational system lost the quickening influence it possessed in the sixteenth century, not because Greek literature and art are any less fresh and beautiful, but because the system ignored the motives and ideas, contained in Greek civilisation, of which Greek literature and art were the expression. The sixteenth century, when the influence of Greek literature and art was so powerfully felt in

Europe, was the crest of a great intellectual and artistic wave which passed over the whole civilised world, affecting India, Persia, China, and Japan, almost as much as it did Italy and other European countries. Even in the fifteenth and sixteenth centuries the literature and art of Greece were an influence only, not the source of inspiration. They were the quickening influence in the Renaissance in Italy, because the intellectual and social conditions of the time were in many ways analogous to those which had given them birth in ancient Greece, not from an inherent creative power contained in themselves, as modern pedagogy would have us believe. But the educational traditions of the pseudo-classic school have still many followers, and the English public-school boy is too often fed on the husks of Greek literature, in the belief that style is the only end of literary expression. The usual art teaching in English public schools is just as remote from the spirit of Greek philosophy. Art, according to modern pedagogy, is merely a fashionable taste for water-colour landscape painting, and with more or less skill in this elegant accomplishment most Englishmen are ready to decide all artistic questions. In the schoolboy's after-life this rigid adherence to forms without principles, and fashions without motives, degraded nineteenth-century art as much as it degraded social life. The training of the artist and architect was based on a slavish imitation of effete schools and defunct styles. The living art of the Greeks applied to practical life the principles of perfect order, perfect arrangement, perfect workmanship, and perfect fitness for use, which are always found in Nature's work and regulate all healthy styles of art. Beauty was sought after not merely for its own sake, but because to the Greeks absolute beauty was absolute perfection. But the nineteenth century forsook the cult of the beautiful for the cult of the golden calf. So much of the art of the greater part of the nineteenth century as really entered into the life of the nation, and was not relegated to museums and picture galleries, was generally devoid of reality and life; it was vulgar ostentation when it was not rampant ugliness, insipidity and inanity when it was not a cloak for stupid construction or dishonest workmanship.

It is the supreme merit of the new movement in art (by which I do not mean any particular sect or clique, but the general revolt against dead academic formulæ) that, in spite of the eccentricities and extravagances which attend all great transitions, it has brought life and sincerity into the teaching and practice of art. It has taught that style in art is the exoteric expression of an esoteric meaning, and that to separate the one from the other is to divorce the body from the soul. It has taught that neither the Greeks nor the Romans nor the master-minds of the Middle Ages have exhausted all the resources of art, which must always seek the form of expression best adapted to the thoughts and necessities of the times. And, above all, it has taught that art is not a curiosity for museums, but a beneficent influence in public and private life; not a fashion but a faculty; not the privilege of a caste, but a divine gift to humanity.

India, unfortunately, affords another example of the difference between theory and practice, for the conditions which exist in India are in every way favourable for putting into practice the theories of Greek philosophy which English higher education professes to take for its gospel. India is the only part of the British Empire where the æsthetic sense of the people, in spite of all that British philistinism has done to suppress it, strongly influences their every day life. It is pitiful to find, even in semi-European cities like Bombay and Calcutta—where nine out of ten of the imposing public buildings built for the official administration flaunt before the native gaze the banalities and vulgarities of the worst English nineteenth-century architecture—that one may go into a back slum and see a modern Mahomedan mosque or Hindu temple, in which the native workman, in naive admiration, has borrowed the details from these Gothic or Classic atrocities, and contrived by the unconscious exercise of his inner æsthetic consciousness to build something which defies all the musty canons of scholastic architectural law, but yet reveals something of that essential spirit of beauty which all living art possesses. In places more remote from European influence, the houses, mosques and temples built by native workmen of the present day, who have had no other education than the traditions of their fathers, are hardly less eloquent than the nobler monuments of the past in their silent protest against the stupid materialism and the false classicism with which the art of the West would instruct the art of the East.

Perhaps the greatest fault to be found with our educational methods in India is in their lack of imagination. Following the traditions of the English Public School we have always regarded the schoolboy as an animal in which the imaginative faculties should be sternly repressed. Build a barrack in the heart of a dirty, overcrowded city, pack it with students—that is a college. Cram the students with Shakespeare and Milton before they can express their own ideas in tolerable modern English—that is culture. It would appear from the evidence given before Lord Curzon's Universities Commission that there are still many exponents of this kind of education flourishing under the shelter of our Indian Universities. Greatly concerned for the lack of moral principle in the generation newly fledged under their own protection, some Indian educational authorities have for many years been seeking a moral text-book as a remedy for the evil. They are still vainly looking for that text-book, though India has a very old one and a very good one, which has served the world for many ages. Plato found it twenty-three centuries ago—'*To use the beauties of earth as steps along which he mounts upwards.*' Our forefathers knew it when they built the most famous of our seats of learning and joined the resources of art to the richest of Nature's endowments. Darwin, in the nineteenth century, proclaimed the scientific truth contained in it, when he taught the influnce of environment upon the development of species.

It is not perhaps astonishing to find that many educationists in India, both native and European, have not risen higher in their conception of education than the routine of instruction which for many generations has been considered the only one suitable for an English gentleman. We have taught English to the Indian schoolboy just as Greek is taught to the English schoolboy. All the accidence, prosody and etymology, which to the average English schoolmaster represent Greek literature and thought, stand for Shakespeare's 'native wood-notes wild' in the mind of the average Indian teacher. And the attitude of Indian educationsts towards art only reflects the universal ideas of the greater part of the nineteenth century not only in England but in the greater part of Europe. But the vital difference between the conditions prevailing in Europe and in India make the consequences of our educational deficiencies and mistakes far more serious to the Indian social system than they are to our own. The Englishman's school career is only one of the many influences which help to form his character and mental development. He has endless opportunities—both during his schooldays and afterwards—of supplying for himself the wants of his individual aptitudes and tendencies which his school-training leaves unsatisfied. The public-school system, with all its shortcomings, at least leaves him with a *mens sana in corpore sano*, free and eager to fight the battle of life. The same cannot always be said for higher education in India. The ordinary Indian schoolboy, directly he leaves his vernacular studies and enters upon his University course, finds himself in an entirely artificial environment of ideas in which even his teachers are often helpless to guide him. Certainly there is a small proportion of students whose families for several generations have lived in close intercourse with European society and have adopted more or less English ways of living. Such students begin their regular English studies under much more favourable conditions, for they have learnt to speak English and to imbibe English ideas almost from childhood. But the great majority of Indian students have little or nothing outside the four walls of their Schoolhouse or College to aid them in finding their way along the bewildering paths of European thought. Less resourceful and less active than their English fellows, as Indian schoolboys generally are, it, is not surprising, when they discover so little food for their reflective and imaginative faculties in the mental fare provided for them, that they should be quite content to let the most precious part of their intellectual possessions lie fallow and only cultivate that which promises the surest and easiest way of obtaining their academic diplomas—namely, a retentive memory. Spending the best part of their schooldays in dingy and dirty class-rooms and in the squalor of even dingier and dirtier lodgings, with little or nothing of the distractions which help to make the English boy's schooldays the happiest time of his life, their brains constantly racked in the endeavour to assimilate what the incompetence or indifference of their teachers often reduces to a meaningless jargon of words, there need be little wonder that so many finish their school career with no other ambition and no other hope than to find at last some comfortable harbour for cerebral inertia in a Government or private office.

Yet, however much some of our educational methods may be open to criticism, it must always be allowed that in the introduction of a system of higher education, based upon the teaching of a language and ideas entirely foreign to the people, there have been extraordinary difficulties. The intellectual gifts which make a really great teacher are as rare as a four-leaved shamrock, and it is hardly the fault of the Indian Education Department, with its huge organisation, that it has not been able to grow enough for its requirements. Its weakest points, perhaps, have been those which are the common failings of all Government Departments—too great reliance on cut and dried systems and too little attention to the quality and training of its Executive officers. But I fear that history will not judge the treatment of the artistic side of education in India with the same indulgence, for on the one hand we have neglected the most magnificent opportunity, and on the other hand countenanced and encouraged the most ruthless barbarity. Even the Goths and Vandals in their most ferocious iconoclasm did less injury to art than that which we have done and continue to do in the name of European civilisation. If the Goths and Vandals destroyed, they brought with them the genius to reconstruct. But we, a nation whose æsthetic understanding has been deadened by generations of pedantry and false teaching, have done all that indifference and active philistinism could do to suppress the lively inborn artistic sense of the Indian peoples. All that recent Indian administrations have done to support and encourage art is but a feather in the scale against the destructive counter-influences, originating in times less sympathetic to Indian art which have been allowed to continue under their authority.

Schools of Art have been established in the four chief Presidency Cities, but they have been left so much to their own devices that for thirty years the teaching in two of them ignored the very existence of any indigenous art. For several years past one of the largest has devoted itself almost entirely to the manufacture of aluminium cooking-vessels, and this year another new enterprise in the application of art to modern life evoked from the controlling authority of this school the expression of a pious doubt as to whether experimenting in aero-motors was the proper function of a School of Art!

Government subsidies have been given to Art Exhibitions, but with so little discrimination or definite purpose that, instead of encouraging the highest possible standard of design and workmanship—the only justification of State aid—they have helped to degrade Indian art, and in the long run to injure it commercially, by advertising the inferior productions manufactured only for the European and American markets. Though large sums have been spent in building and maintaining them, there is hardly an Art Museum in India which has had qualified artistic advice in the purchase of its collections. These, however, are merely ordinary symptoms of nineteenth-century incapacity to deal seriously and sanely with art questions; and however well managed they might be, four Schools of Art, a half dozen Museums, and an occasional Exhibition could not affect very deeply the artistic sense of three hundred million people. If art had ever been considered of sufficient importance in India to engage the serious attention of responsible administrators, we should never have placed any great reliance upon the artificial stimulants which the low vitality of our æsthetic constitutions renders necessary in Europe. For the one conspicuous fact which must force itself upon the attention of any one who seriously studies the artistic condition of India is that in the real India, which exists outside the semi-Europeanised society we have created, art belongs as much to the everyday-life of the people as it did in ancient Greece. In Europe we play with art as a child plays with a toy, not knowing its use except as a plaything. The artist is a specialist who is called in by those who can afford to pay for the amusement; but art is always more or less a frivolity which serious and sensible people dispense with as much as possible, except when it happens to be fashionable. In the Hindu social organisation there are no Schools of Art, no Art Museums, but art lives and is felt as much by the ryot as by the maharajah. In the typical Hindu village every carpenter, mason, potter blacksmith, brass-smith, and weaver is an artist, and the making of cooking-pots is as much an artistic and religious work as the building of the village temple. So throughout our vast Indian Empire there is a most marvellous store of artistic material available for educational and economic purposes, such as exists nowhere in Europe.

How have we used this extraordinary opportunity for restoring the real classic ideal of education which the youth of England fondly regard as their own? The answer given by the schools, public buildings and streets of Anglo-Indian towns and cities should make us ashamed of nineteenth-century civilisation.

The great national educator in art, that which brings

art home to us and makes it live with us—namely, the architecture of the country—we have practically converted in India into a Government monopoly. Thus, for the last fifty years at least, we have had at hand a really effective instrument by which, without spending an extra rupee, without Schools of Art, without Art Museums, and without Exhibitions, we could have stimulated the whole artistic intelligence of the people and brought prosperity to the principal art industries. This intrument we have deliberately thrown away. Let us examine this point carefully. In European architecture of the last few centuries there has gradually grown up a hard and fast distinction between architecture and building—the same false distinction which is commonly made between artistic work and useful work. The natural consequence was that the builder became less and less an architect, and the architect less and less a builder. Gradually the builder became an unintelligent tool in the hands of the architect, and the architect, instead of evolving artistic ideas from structural necessities, came to regard his art either as a screen for concealing the ugliness of construction or as a means of forcing construction into certain conventional moulds which he wrongly called 'styles.' With the total loss of artistic expression in building which we reached in the middle of the nineteenth century, European architecture degenerated into a confused jumble of archæological ideas borrowed from the buildings of former times. In India, on the other hand, architecture has continued to be a living art down to the present day, because there building and architecture are always one. The master-mason is both builder and architect, just as he was in Europe in the Middle Ages. Over a great part of Northern India there still exist descendants of the master-builders of the Mogul period, practising their art as it was practised in the days of Akbar, Jahangir, and Shah Jahan. If they do not now produce anything to compare with the masterpieces of those days, how could it be expected under the conditions which our shortsighted policy imposes upon them? For ever since we have created a Government monopoly in architecture, we have totally ignored these men, who could teach us more of the art of building than we could teach them; we have boycotted them and the art industries dependent upon them, and have foisted upon India the falsest of our nineteenth-century art, which means nothing and teaches nothing, and is utterly unworthy of the dignity and intelligence of the English nation.

What Fergusson wrote nearly thirty years ago in his *History of Indian and Eastern Architecture* is almost as true now as it was then:

Architecture in India is still a living art, practised on the principles which caused its wonderful development in Europe in the twelfth and thirteenth centuries, and there consequently and there alone, the student of architecture has a chance of seeing the real principles of the art in action. In Europe, at the present day, architecture is practised in a manner so anomalous and so abnormal that few, if any, have hitherto been able to shake off the influence of a false system and see that the art of ornamental building can be based on principles of common sense, and that when so practisd the result not only is, but must be, satisfactory.

What a tremendous impetus we should have given to Indian art had we only made a sensible use of the men who thus carry on the living traditions of architecture when we spent the many crores of rupees which have been sunk in the so-called imposing public buildings of Bombay and Calcutta! What an object-lesson those cities might have been both to ourselves and to the rest of the Empire! Are these indigenous styles of India all unsuitable for our requirements in building? No one will imagine that who tries to appreciate the essential difference between a living and an academic style of architecture. The modern European architect, when he is designing holds up to his mind, either consciously or unconsciously, some ancient building or buildings as patterns to imitate. This is why we so often see theatres like Greek temples, hospitals like churches, and suburban villas like mediæval castles. The original designers of these pattern buildings very rarely thought of imitating any thing else. They were taught now to build and having learnt, they made their buildings suitable for the purposes for which they were intended, without any thought of the buildings their ancestors had made for their own purposes. It is exactly the same with the modern Indian architect. It is unreasonable to suppose that such past masters in the art of building as the Moguls showed themselves to be, could not have designed a hospital, police station, railway station, or any other accessory of modern life, as well as they built a palace, mosque, or mausoleum. No one can suppose that they would have been so stupid as we are and make a hospital like a mosque or a town-hall like a mausoleum. Neither is it reasonable to assume that that the descendants of these men, who still carry on their traditions, could not understand our requirements if we attempted to teach them or give them the opportunity of learning. But the Indian Public Works engineers, with a few exceptions, have never attempted to study the architecture of the country and have always worked on the blind assumption that the native architects have only built temples and mosques, forgetting that we ourselves have destroyed, or allowed to decay, most of the civil buildings which the Mogul and other Indian architects constructed.

But how, it may be asked, does this architectural

question affect the problem of general education? Because, until the art education of India is put upon a sane and practical basis, art can never take the place it ought to take in a thorough system of general education. As long as the great Government building department in India uses its whole influence to stifle the artistic sentiments of the people, it stultifies all that is being done or might be done educationally in a different direction. For every one who knows India is aware what a powerful influence Government initiative has upon popular feeling. In England, if the Government were to adopt ancient Egyptian or Babylonian architectural ideas in the designs of public offices, it is highly improbable that the Royal Institute of British Architects would make the practice of these styles compulsory on its members, or that the general public would follow official example. But in India official authority controls the fashion in architecture, as in many other things, especially in the more advanced or more Europeanised provinces. The Engineering Colleges in India follow the example of Cooper's Hill in teaching only European styles, and even European architects who are not in Government service are obliged by force of circumstances to adopt the official fashion. So the native hereditary builder has been deprived of all official and a great deal of non-official patronage unless he has forsaken the art of his forefathers and blindly followed his blind European leaders. Consequently also the wood-carvers, stone-carvers, painters, and all the other craftsmen connected directly or indirectly with architecture (a category which includes nearly all the industrial arts) find the principle source of employment cut off from them. Thus do we, in the name of European culture and civilisation, crush out the artistic feeling of the Indian peoples.

What then are the necessary steps to take in order to put the Indian educational system on a better footing with regard to art teaching ? For, if we really believe in the teaching of Greek philosophy and Greek civilisation we must be convinced that it is no real education which does not help to develop all the higher imaginative faculties. First, we must accept the principle which the Greeks acted upon, that which has been acknowledged more or less in every country, though in the nineteenth century we tried to ignore it—namely, the influence of environment on the development of mind and character. The greatness or meanness of men's motives is reflected in the surroundings they make for themselves; and inversely, if we educate young India to mean and ignoble surroundings we must not expect great things from them, either respect for us or respect for themselves. We can doubt that the situation of Eton College, with all its noble surroundings in that lovely part of the Thames Valley which is the delight of every artist, has had a great influence for good—not the less profound because it cannot be gauged by examinations—on the mind and character of those who have had the advantage of learning in the most famous of English schools! Eton is not an isolated example; most of the old English Schools and Colleges are distinguished both by architectural beauty and by the beauty of their surroundings. Though it cannot be stated in definite terms or calculated by statistics, the whole English nation benefits spiritually, morally, and intellectually by the wisdom and loving care of our forefathers when they built the old Schools and Colleges of which we are justly proud. If we had shown more of the same wisdom and care in our educational efforts in India, the feeble shoot of Western culture which we have been trying to graft upon the ancient civilisation of the country might by now have been a more vigorous branch. There are many Colleges and Schools connected with Indian Universities in which the most ordinary necessities and decencies of school-life are hardly attended to. A short time ago the Vice-Chancellor of the Bombay University referred in a lecture to certain schools in Upper India in which, he said, everything was fitted to depress the minds of the students: the rooms that were there were destitute of proper light, destitute of every kind of reasonable appliances, and yet these institutions rejoiced in a high-sounding title and were recognised by the University. I think every one will agree with the Vice-Chancellor's view that it would be better to conduct a High School under the shadow of a banyan tree than in such places as these, for much of the ancient culture of India has grown up under banyan trees. Such cases as these may be extreme, but hardly anywhere in India—certainly not in Bengal—has it yet been accepted as an axiom that education has a great concern in choosing or arranging harmonious surroundings for Schools and Colleges.

When we have attended to the surroundings of schools, let us turn our attention to the buildings and try to free our minds from the popular fallacy that art is an expensive luxury. Art is a luxury with us, only because we in our foolishness have made it so. In India art is no luxury; it is the common property of the poorest and the richest. The art of the peasant is just as real and just as true as the art of the greatest maharajah. We practise no economy, but the most reckless wastefulness, when we check the natural development of Indian art and architecture and surround Indian students with all the ugliness Europe produced in the nineteenth century. Set Indian art free to follow its natural channel, remove the impediments we have placed in its course, and it can minister to the spiritual and intellectual needs of India and at the same time increase the prosperity of the people and add to the resources of the State. And when we have provided Indian students with an environment which will help to elevate their moral and intellectual faculties, let us try in every way to stimulate their love for what is beautiful in nature and in art. The Government of India and some of the Local Governments publish from time to time many excellent illustrations of Indian art and architecture, which in India, at least, serve no other purpose than to help to fill the almirahs of Government Offices. Such illustrations might be used to brighten the class-rooms and corridors of Indian Schools and Colleges, and to accustom the eyes of students to beautiful things. Let us get rid of that false culture which reduces education to a dull system of mental gymnastics, which crams an Indian undergraduate with Shakespeare's plays, but leaves him ignorant of everything in heaven and earth that Shakespeare included in his philosophy. It is not education, but the most pernicious pedantry, which uses Western culture to blind the eyes and stop the ears of Indian youth to all that the nature, the art, and the culture of their own country have to teach them.

With regard to methods of direct art teaching, an intelligent system of instruction in Drawing should not only develop the powers of observation but teach students to appreciate beauty of form and line. We should by all means avoid in India the mistake so frequently made in English public schools through which art education comes to mean amateur picture-painting. Picture-painting holds precisely the same place in art that novel-writing and poetry hold in literature. I imagine that no serious educationist would ever propose to make practice in writing novels or poems the principal part of literary exercise in public schools. The increase in the number of minor novelists and minor poets which such a system would produce is too alarming to contemplate. It is only another proof of the incapacity of our generation to take art seriously that we should have ever adopted such a method of art-teaching as a part of a general education.

When students have been taught to observe and their hands have been practised in Drawing, I know of no better way of developing their artistic perception than the practice of elementary design. Design is the foundation of all art practice, and, properly taught, it is not only a very fascinating study, but it tends to healthier and wider views of art than sketching in oils and water-colours.

The Indian student has a great natural aptitude for ornamental design which can be easily developed. I have always made a point of including elementary design in the course for the native Drawing teachers trained under me in the Madras and Calcutta Schools of Art, and I have seen some excellent work done by the pupils of these teachers in some of the Madras Colleges.

I believe that work of this kind is educationally valuable, even though the students after vocation may be only to fill up official forms or to write objection statements. To understand beauty, to enjoy it and feel that it is necessary for us, is surely not merely idle gratification. The whole history of mankind shows how generation after generation of every race strives, consciously or unconsciously, to understand beauty. It is a struggle to lift ourselves into a higher plane of intelligence, to obtain in this life some dim knowledge of one of the eternal laws on which the universe is constructed, a presentiment of that Nirvana of perfect beauty of which Plato wrote, on which all the hopes of humanity are fixed.—*Nineteenth Century and After*, *February*, 1903.

II.

The educational branch of the Indian administration has not, on the whole, been conspicuous for its successes. After many experiments and failures, it may be said to be adapting itself gradually to the peculiar and diverse conditions of the country, but it has hardly yet passed through the experimental stage, and many of the mistakes of its first organisation have yet to be remedied. For years England herself lagged far behind many European nations in educational matters, and it was only human, therefore, that Indian administrators, overburdened with all the complicated and delicate problems connected with the government of the Empire, should fail to achieve a conspicuous success in a question the mother-country had so much neglected. But there is this peculiarity about art education in India, that whereas, in every other department of the service, profit has been derived from failures and progress evolved from mistakes, this one alone seems to be always enveloped in difficulty and doubt, without a prospect of enlightenment, and always the subject of discussions ending in the most lame and impotent conclusions. This is the more extraordinary, since in India the general conditions are altogether favourable for art progress. Ever since the dawn of history, India has been known as the nursery of art, and, before the British rule was established, the artistic instincts of the people have never been suppressed. Every religious sect—Brahmin, Jain, Buddhist, Sikh or Mahomedan—have left their mark on the art of the country; all the conquering hordes, which, century after century, swept down from the North and ravaged the country, have brought art in their train and written the history of their times in masterpieces which will ever remain the admiration of the world. We have established a peace such as India has never known before Liberty of the subject, law and order, material progress, in fact, all the first conditions favourable to the development of art, among a people whose traditions and instincts are always artistic—all these we have established in the India of to-day; why is it, then, that the last half century, so far from being a great art epoch, finds Indian art year by year becoming more corrupt and degraded?

No one who knows India well can fail to see how the taste of the native aristocracy and plutocracy has been utterly vitiated; how indigenous architecture has become almost extinct; how the art handicrafts of the country are only explcited for the sake of gain by the Philistine dealer, whose standard of taste is regulated by the demands of tourists and curiosity-hunters. Indian art has fallen into such disrepute among the natives themselves that everything which does not come straight from Europe is looked upon as something inferior. The native nobility affect a taste for the Brummagem art we have introduced into the country, and a sentimental passion for spurious Old Masters supplied to them at fancy prices by unscrupulous agents and picture dealers. What remains to-day of the real, living art of India must be looked for in out of the way places, and is regarded by the natives as old fashioned and behind the times. Even the curiosity dealer finds his business not what it used to be. The not too discriminating taste of the globe-trotter is getting rather nauseated with the commonplace bric-a-brac which is palmed off upon him as Indian art, and even the glamour of the gorgeous East hardly spreads a halo of romance over the crude and tasteless ornament manufactured for the European and American market. The painful fact must be admitted, that, whatever the cause may be, since our rule has been established, the old art of India has been almost killed; the taste of the people, formerly led into safe paths by the traditions of Indian handicraftsmen, has been changed and corrupted, while we have given nothing from our own national art to compensate India for what has been lost.

This is not an exaggerated picture of the present

state of art in India. The facts have been more or less fully realised by the Indian Government for some time past. The causes which have produced such a state of things have been far less perfectly understood. Generally the question has been treated more from the standpoint of a municipal council than as a matter of great imperial concern, and though it has been dealt with in innumerable despatches, resolutions, reports of committees and other documents, hardly anything but vague suggestions and rhetorical platitudes have ever come out of them. Of late years the general drift of policy has been to treat Indian art as something too abstruse and mysterious to be interfered with, even for saving it from annihilation. But as a scape-goat must always be found, when the wheels of official administration do not run smoothly, the Indian Schools of Art have most unjustly been held responsible for a state of things which they could never, under the most favourable conditions, have prevented. For how could four Schools of Art, separated from each other by many hundreds of miles and under different Administrations, which have never yet been able to decide a definite and continuous policy for the development of art education, be expected to effect a revolution in the art feeling of 350,000,000 people, or to influence, to any appreciable extent, those adverse conditions which in the nature of things must have been very deep-seated and wide-spreading to have produced such disastrous effects on the art of the whole country? Whether the Schools of Art have been as successful as they might have been is quite beside the question. Certainly, within the scope which has been allowed them and in spite of many disadvantages, they have accomplished a great deal of solid, useful work, but no reasonable being, acquainted with the real condition of things in India, would ever believe for a moment that the salvation of Indian art depended solely on the efficiency or inefficiency of the Schools of Art at present existing.

Indian art was certainly in a state of decadence before the British ascendancy, but we need hardly look for any other explanation of this than in the political unrest, internal disorganisation, disorder and misgovernment which accompanied the dissolution of the Mogul Empire. When these causes were removed, one would naturally expect that art would have revived under the benign influence of the "pax Brittanica." No doubt there were some influences, originating with the very foundations of our Indian rule and long before we had any pretence of a policy in art education, which, the more British influence predominated, acted more and more injuriously on art in India. One of these was the circumstance that Madras, Bombay and Calcutta, the centres from which the ascendancy of our rule radiated over the whole of India, were not centres of Indian art. The early settlers of the old John Company were in no way concerned, as is the Government of India to-day, in the administration of a great Empire. They were hard-headed merchants absorbed in their own affairs, which were the development of the Company's trade and the protection of their lands and factories. There were no reasons of State why they should concern themselves with the influence their example might have on Indian art. It pleased their national pride and kept alive home memories to retain the architectural style then fashionable in the country mansions, public offices and churches of England, and to imitate, as far as conditions of climate would permit, the life of the old country. When our influence became paramount in India, the style and standard of taste thus created in the capital cities became the model for all the native aristocracy under our protection. With the native princes it became the mark of modern culture and a sign of sympathy with the British domination to build and furnish their palaces in the same style. This was the beginning of the degradation of Indian art, for nothing more hopelessly irreconcilable with Oriental ideas of art could ever have been adopted than the cold, formal classicism then fashionable in England. It was the greatest misfortune for India that, at the time when the foundations of our Indian administration were laid, the national taste in England had sunk to the lowest depths. It was the time when Westminster Abbey and St. Paul's were being filled with those horrors in marble, intended to glorify the deeds of the great departed, which still disfigure those two noble monuments of English art; when the old art handicrafts of the country were being almost extinguished by the crushing competition of machine-made products, and when all individuality in architecture and the fine arts was drowned in a vapid affectation of classic taste.

It may be doubted, however, whether, even if art taste in England at that time had been better than it was, we should ever have arrived immediately at the right appreciation of the policy required for the development of art in India. It is one of our national prejudices that what is good enough for the Anglo-Saxon is good enough for the rest of the world, if not too good. That was the keynote of our policy in educational matters in India, as well as in many other things.

However indifferent to the true interests of the country the Honorable East India Company may have been in their artistic ideas, the old Anglo-Indian architecture had at least this merit—it was the best that England could produce at that time and, in spite of their monotony and baldness, the houses, churches and other buildings of fifty years ago and older are not without a certain grim solemnity and dignity, in keeping with the prim fashions of the time and suggestive of the character of their occupants, while the honesty of purpose of the builders is shown by the strict regard to comfort and adaptability to the climate with which all the old buildings were designed. Very few modern Anglo-Indian buildings are equal to the old ones in these respects.

Since the Crown assumed the responsibilities of imperial rule, it must be admitted that some progress has been made in art education, though very little has been done to repair the injuries unconsciously inflicted on Indian art by the early settlers of the East India Company. It is a great step gained that in educational matters generally, it is now being recognised that India is a country with an ancient civilisation, literature and art, containing within itself the means of development and requiring different methods of administration to primitive colonies like Australia, New Zealand or "Darkest Africa." The Schools of Art have generally improved upon the crude systems of art education imported from England when they were first instituted, about 50 years ago, but Indian art on the whole still goes on the downward path. The measures which have been devised or proposed to arrest its decay amount to very little. Though Indian statesmen are always deploring the decline of native industries, it has never yet occurred to them that the degradation of popular sentiment in art may be an important factor in this great question. As long as art is regarded only as a hobby, a means of distraction from the worries of serious official duties, but not a subject of sufficient importance for the close personal attention of those who have the heavy care of Government on their shoulders, so long will Indian art continue to decay. The practical British mind looks to railways, canals, roads, bridges, famine prevention, sanitation and police, and the development of mills, factories and warehouses as the chief means of India's regeneration. Art is a mere question of sentiment which may be left for a more convenient question. Perhaps the artists of the nineteenth century are themselves greatly to blame for the attitude which the British public has taken in regarding art as only a subject for society functions and drawing-room conversation, to be put aside in the serious work of every-day life. Art in the present century has been too much of a sham, and the general public, seeing the deception, have fallen back on pure utilitarianism, preferring honest ugliness to pretentious art. If art in England during the last quarter of a century has begun to assert itself again, to some extent, as an essential part of our national life, it is only because the better education of our artists and art workers of all classes has begun to convince the public that the elementary basis and justification of all technic art lies in the ultimate perfection of utility, and that even the highest forms of art gain in dignity from being associated with a utilitarian purpose.

Modern Indian art is corrupt and decaying, because for the most part it has lost hold of the sentiment of the people of the country. It is like English art of fifty years ago, affected and insincere. No art can ever flourish if the national sentiment is not in it. To find the causes which have led to the decay of Indian art we must, therefore, first investigate the reasons for this degradation of popular sentiment. At first thought any one who is not closely acquainted with Indian affairs might imagine that the explanation is easily to be found in the changed political conditions of the country. It might be argued plausibly that, as the art of every country has its periods of rise and decay, so India under the domination of the practical and unsentimental Anglo-Saxon now turns its attention to purely industrial pursuits and looks less to the imaginative and spiritual side of life. Against this argument we have the indisputable facts, which Indian statesmen are always deploring, that the proportion of the artisan to the rest of the population is either stationary or steadily diminishing, and that the native capitalist is even now very shy of any industrial undertaking, preferring to invest his money in landed property or in usury. Further more Indian art in all times before the British rule has always shown a wonderful power of assimilating foreign influences, whether drawn from Europe or Asia. What then is the reason for the apparent blighting influence of the last fifty years on the art of India?

The history of the art of every country is contained in the history of its architecture, at least in countries where architecture has reached the dignity of an art. Every national movement in art has first formed expression in building. A decline in architecture means a decline in national taste, and thus when architecture decays the rest of the arts suffer with it. The general truth of this proposition every student of art will admit. Architecture has given birth to all the arts of the painter and sculptor, the carver and inlayer of wood and stone, the glass painter, the plasterer, the gesso, or lacquer worker, and other minor arts, while it has exercised an enormous influence on the development of other arts, such as those of the weaver, potter and workers in iron-bronze, brass and other metals

When, therefore, we begin to enquire into the causes of the decay of Indian art, the first and most important question to be asked is—how has British rule affected the architecture of the country? The answer to this question is the key to the whole difficulty. It is astonishing that in all the official enquiries which have been held this point has been hardly alluded to. Committees and Commissions innumerable have been appointed to enquire into mere side issues, such as the working of the Schools of Art, and for some years past the whole discussion has been centred upon the merits or demerits of these four institutions. It is not surprising therefore that such beating about the bush has ended in nothing save an accumulation of paper in Government offices. The Secretary of State, in despair, once proposed to abolish the schools altogether, or, what would have been worse, to place them under municipal control, thus practically washing his hands of the whole affair and leaving Indian art severely alone.

It has been pointed out above how, even in the early days of the John Company, Anglo-Indian taste or want of taste in architecture had set an evil influence over Indian art. But the evil was perpetuated and intensified a hundredfold when, on the formation of the Department of Public Works, the Government instituted what was practically a monopoly of the whole civil architecture of the country. That in itself might have done no harm if those who organised the Department had reflected that by this monopoly the Government practically took into their own hands the future of Indian art. But so little were the interests of art understood or cared for, so little were Indian administrators then concerned with the most obvious teachings of art history, that in organising the department practically no provision was made for training any of its officers as architects. Architecture, in the Indian Public Works system, has always been treated as a minor branch of Civil Engineering; it could not be otherwise in a course of training, only of 3 or 4 years' duration, combining both engineering and architecture. Indian styles are not recognised as architecture at all. Even in European styles the mere smattering of architectural grammar, such as committing to memory the five classic orders and the forms of Gothic mouldings, which is the most the Public Works officer acquires at College, is worse than useless to him, for it leads him off the path he ought to go when he comes to India. The inevitable result of this system of training is that minor architectural works, which the young officer has to supervise when he first comes to India, are regulated by a sealed-pattern, machine-made, departmental style, which has been evolved out of a long series of departmental mistakes, leaving as little as possible to the discretion or indiscretion of the officer. The more important architectural works, such as are found in the large towns, are handed over to any senior engineer, either one who has had special opportunities or has shown a predilection for architectural design, improved and developed by a course of experimenting on Government buildings. The horrors which have been perpetrated in the name of architecture under this happy-go-lucky system it is needless to particularise. They offend the eye and haunt the imagination in every station of India from Simla, Calcutta and Bombay down to the smallest mofussil town. Of course, there have been exceptional men, self-taught, architecturally speaking, who have overcome the disadvantages and difficulties in which they are placed by the departmental system, but even these, as a rule, have only striven to excel in architectural design as it was understood in England before the present revival in art began, and have failed entirely to appreciate the immense resources, now going to waste, which

India places in the hands of architects and designers who know and are willing to make use of them.

It is no disparagement of the splendid and devoted services done for India by the Public Works engineers in their own special branch to say that this treatment of the noblest of all the arts is unworthy of England's reputation as a great civilising power, and unworthy of the great mission she has set herself to achieve in India. It is the ruin of Indian art and a source of great material loss to the country, which can and should be avoided. We give with one hand and take away with the other. We build splendid railways, roads and bridges, we dig canals and irrigate hundreds of thousands of acres, prevent famines or strive to alleviate suffering when they occur, but on the other hand we corrupt the artistic sentiment of the people, and by so doing cause the ruin of the ancient handicrafts which have always been the pride of India. Fortunately for art, in some parts of India, notably in Rajputana, Central India and the Punjab, the natives have shown themselves more independent and less imitative of European fashions than in Bengal, Madras and other more modernised provinces. Generally speaking, with the "educated" or English speaking natives, art is not an individual feeling—it is merely a fashion, and when the fashion they imitate is only that set by the Public Works engineers, it is easy to understand that the hopes of raising the standard of their taste are not promising.

Most of the Princes and rich men of India, when they require a new palace or mansion, requisition the services of a Public Works officer, who designs a pretentious edifice in the Anglo-Indian style. So instead of affording occupation to a small army of the hereditary art workmen of India—wood carvers, stone carvers, fresco painters, inlayers of wood and stone, potters and others innumerable—each of these buildings is handed over to a set of workmen trained, in the traditions of the Public Works Department to copy mechanically from working drawings things without beauty, and to pile up a mass of brick or stone, without any sort of artistic expression, testifying only in size and empty display to the vanity of its occupier. The furnishing of the building must follow the same style; the walls must be hung with European pictures and the rooms upholstered with European carpets and furniture by the most fashionable European firms. This is typical of what has been going on ever since our rule was established in India. Is it a wonder that Indian art decays, and that the old handicraftsmen are driven to agriculture for an occupation? The whole system strikes at the very foundation of art, and unless it is altered the entire ruin of Indian art is inevitable.

Some people suppose, when they see the considerable trade in bric-à-brac and so-called curiosities, which has resulted from the Great International Exhibitions in Europe and America, that Indian art has found a new market abroad to compensate for the loss of the old one at home. But can any one imagine for a moment that arts which have been created by the spontaneous sentiment of a people, finding its first and chief expression in architecture, can ever thrive and develop by the manufacture of cheap curiosities for foreign export?

The first condition for the healthy development of art is its sincerity. Sincerity, as Lord Leighton said at the first meeting of the Society for the Encouragement and Preservation of Indian art in 1891, is the true element of life in art. In these Indian curiosities there is no sincerity; for the workmen who manufacture them on contract they have no meaning; for the purchasers they are only curiosities. Those who have been able to compare the standard of design and workmanship in all branches of Indian art exhibited at the great Exhibition of 1851, with recent exhibitions know well how great the falling off has been. Quite apart from any question of artistic merit or sentiment, the new export markets which have been opened for the Indian workman are not a hundredth part of the home market which has been for the most part closed to him. It is futile to argue that the splendid engineering works of the Public Works Department more than compensate for the injuries done to Indian art. That is quite beside the question. The fault is that we impose upon the Public Works engineers a double responsibility and only train them for a single one.

It is necessary to point out why, from an artistic point of view, the preservation of the living styles of Indian architecture is necessary for the preservation of a healthy and vigorous life in Indian art. Many of the art workmen of India who have not been driven to agriculture for a livelihood, or have not been converted into ignorant copyists of Public Works patterns, exist chiefly by the manufacture of bric-a-brac for the European market. Let us consider for a moment the conditions under which they work. They make tea tables, tea trays and table covers, chairs, brackets, vases and "curiosities," on contract with the dealers in such wares. The dealers care nothing for the artistic excellence of what they sell; whatever will catch the popular taste is to them the most desirable, and it is hardly necessary to say that the contract system as worked by them is not conducive to high artistic effort. The workmen are mere drudges; their commerical instincts and not their artistic faculties are developed by the work they are compelled to do. How different it was when the architecture which created their art afforded it nourishment and support. They worked in a congenial atmosphere and were continually spurred to higher efforts by a spirit of artistic emulation. Their work was not something which was shipped off to Europe and never seen again. If a man did a fine piece of carving it was discussed and criticised by his fellow-workmen, it became the talk of the bazaar and one of the sights of the town, and remained for succeeding generations to admire and imitate. If a private house or palace was to be decorated the owner took a personal interest in the work and encouraged the workmen, for he felt a pride in the adornment of his home and the home of his family. An exact illustration is given in a report by Mr. J. L. Kipling on the Punjab Exhibition of 1881-82. He says:—"In building a house, for example, the work people are all paid wages more or less regularly, but for any extra spurt or during the execution of delicate or difficult details they are often liberally treated with sweetmeats, tobacco, sharbat, etc. In some districts when a carpenter has made a carven *chaukut* for door or window he takes a holiday to exhibit it, and spreading a sheet on the ground lays it down in front of the house it is to adorn, and sits there to receive the congratulations and gifts of his admiring townsmen. As much as Rs. 100 have in one day, been thrown to the carver of a particularly good piece of work." By such means the artistic sense both of the people and of the workmen was kept alive. The present Public Works system dries up the springs of artistic sentiment and checks their flow at the very source. It does not require a very strong imagination to understand that the one system develops the artistic sense of the people and creates a class of good art workmen, and the other turns all artisans into mechanical drudges.

The question often arises—is it not an artistic anomaly to introduce Indian styles into European purposes, in the semi-European cities of India? This is one of those peculiar archæological scruples of the modern art critic which artists and architects of all periods previous to the nineteenth century have resolutely ignored, and surely the artistic and architectural achievements of the nineteenth century are not so great as to justify it in setting up any new canons or principles of taste. One of the most striking characteristics of a healthy and vigorous style of art or architecture has always been its readiness, even anxiety to adopt and assimilate new ideas, and perhaps nothing is more characteristic of the weakness and degeneracy of modern European building styles than the perpetual anxiety of architects over historical correctness. The Renaissance style, which is the style most affected by Anglo-Indians, is in itself a remarkable instance of the contempt with which all the great architects have treated the archæological scruples which so trouble the minds of modern critics, for what more glaring anomaly could be imagined than to take the style of pagan Roman and Greek temples as a model for the Christian churches and palaces of the fifteenth and sixteenth centuries? If art criticism in those days had taken the lines which we generally follow now, the Renaissance style would never have been created. For my part I cannot see why it should be less appropriate to adapt living Indian styles of architecture to our requirements in India than to make a Bombay railway station a grotesque imitation of a Gothic cathedral, or to take Italian palaces as models for the public buildings of Calcutta.

There are many who, while admitting the deficiencies of the present system, argue that this system has been forced upon us by economical necessities. Half a loaf, they say, is better than no bread: the Public Works Department has given India more than half the loaf,

The state cannot afford to employ all these art handicraftsmen in its public works; the country wants plain, economical court houses, hospitals, post offices, police stations and similar works of utility, in which there is no room for art. That art in India cannot be reconciled with economy is the fault of the Public Works Department, not of art. "Ugly is only half way to a thing," says Meredith's "Old Buccaneer" in one of his wise maxims. The Indian Public Works Department believes the other half unattainable because it does not know how to get it. The engineer, as a rule, regards art as synonymous with ornament, to be added more or less lavishly, according to the means at his disposal, when he has finished with his engineering. He has no knowledge of constructive design in architecture, or believes it to be only a matter of calculation, like the thickness of an iron girder. But if the untrained peasant in Italy, and many other parts of the world, can evolve from his inner consciousness, in the infrequent intervals of repose from the labours of cultivation, a style of architecture at once practical, economical, comfortable and pleasing to the eye, into which no vestige of ornament enters, it ought not to be impossible in India to adapt architectural design to the capacity of the public purse. For in India there still exists, unrecognised by the Public Works

Department, a class of native workmen, passing rich on fifteen rupees a month, who are at the same time most skilful builders, decorators and architects. These men are exactly of the same class as the master-builders of the middle ages, to whom we owe the great masterpieces of Gothic architecture; they inherit all the traditions of Indian architecture, they can draw, design, build, carve and decorate, in good taste and with understanding of constructive principles, but they know nothing of Public Works *formulæ* and therefore are held of no account. All this artistic and architectural wealth goes to waste in India because the Public Works Department does not know how to make use of it.

There have been one or two distinguished exceptions of men, like Colonel Jacob at Jeypore, with artistic instincts which have revolted against departmental traditions, who have, by a study and practice of native architecture, done splendid services to Indian art, but individuals do not count for much in India against the established rules of a great Government department. The ordinary Public Works officer ignores altogether the art of the country, and borrows his art and architecture from European professional periodicals, trade catalogues or illustrated works. A typical example will show the injustice done to Indian art in this way. Not many years ago, a number of important buildings were being erected in Calcutta, and for their external decoration terra-cotta to the value of a lakh of rupees was obtained from England. This terra-cotta was not of exceptional artistic merit, to set an example to the Bengalee artisan, but the ordinary commercial ornament which is sold by the square yard by European manufacturers. Now Bengal is a great brick-making country, and there once existed a beautiful art in moulded brick-work, still to be seen in old buildings in many parts of the Province. If a lakh of rupees had been spent in reviving this decayed art, public buildings in Calcutta would have had far better ornament and an old industry might have been revived.

In the same way, through the influence of Anglo-Indian taste, the old process of fresco decoration, in which some of the finest examples of Indian art have been executed during the last 1,000 years, will soon be a lost art, replaced by less sanitary, less durable, and less artistic European wall-papers and hangings. For adapting architectural design to local art it only requires officers with a proper architectural and artistic training. Which is the most economical and statesmanlike policy, to continue to crush out the artistic sentiment of a people by a badly thought out system of department organisation, or to reform that system so as to allow Indian art and industry the scope it had in former times?

What reforms are needed? First, it must be the declared policy of the different Governments to adopt indigenous styles of architecture, as far as possible, in all public buildings. Only to employ professional architects in place of Public Works engineers would not meet the case at all. That has been tried occasionally, and has failed simply because the ordinary European architect in India is too much prejudiced by the pedantries of modern European eclectic architecture to strike out a new path by devoting himself to a study of living Oriental styles. Neither would an improved style of European architecture benefit Indian art, because the average Indian, like the average European, is quite incapable of distinguishing good architecture from bad. What is wanted is a revival of Indian architecture to give an outlet for the hereditary art instincts of Indian handicraftsmen. Oriental architecture should be made a special branch of the Public Works Department. We have established in India schools of medicine, law, agriculture, forestry, engineering and art; why not also architecture? If it were notified that special advantage in pay and promotion would be given to officers of the Public Works Department possessing a diploma in both engineering and architecture, competition for Government appointments is so keen in India that there would be no lack of students. To afford facilities for study, and as a means of instructing the public, museums of architecture should be established in connection with the Colleges of Engineering. The example public buildings might then present would be of far more value to India than the actual monetary aid given to native art in the building of them. When once the native Princes and aristocracy saw that the seal and sign of official approval had been set on Indian architecture, an immense step would be gained. The native *mistri*, or hereditary master-builder, would find that his services were once more sought after; every rich man's mansion or Rajah's palace which was built would afford employment for hundreds of Indian art workmen; art industry restored to its legitimate place would lift up its head again, and art as a whole would prosper and develop, because its foundations rested, not on an obsequious imitation of official styles and fashions, but on the artistic instincts of the people. Art education in India would then at last stand on a firm and rational basis.

It is not to be expected that this consummation would be reached immediately. The mistakes of fifty years cannot be put right in a day, nor is it practicable to pull down and rebuild all the official edifices in Calcutta, Bombay and Madras, which tend to mislead native taste in architecture. But every student of art history, indeed every man of any artistic knowledge, must admit that Indian art would gain more by the restoration of indigenous architecture to its proper position than by any other possible administrative reform. There have no doubt been other and quite different causes which have led to the decay of particular art industries, especially the great weaving industry, but the gradual extinction of native architecture is the great avoidable cause of the degeneration of Indian art. Schools of Art may be developed, art museums may be established, exhibitions may be subsidised, Indian art may be advertised in Europe and America, these are merely as props to a fabric whose foundations are crumbling away.

From a political standpoint it is not a small thing that the artistic sentiment of the Indian peoples is being extinguished under our rule. A people devoted to art are a happy and contented people. A people without art are restless and unhappy. Mrs. Besant in her crusade for promoting religious education among the Hindus has received official countenance and support, because Indian statesmen recognise that the decline of religious belief is a danger to the Empire. The decay of art sentiment is also a danger, for art, if not a part of religion, is a door leading to it. From a commercial standpoint India suffers a heavy loss by the ruin of her art industries. Every ruler who has earned from posterity the title of Great or Wise has spent the resources of the state in encouraging the industrial arts, and money so spent has been well invested, for many states have risen to prosperity and power through the skill of their art handicraftsmen. Art in India, though corrupt and decaying, is still more a part of national life than it is in any European country to-day. Is it not a duty we owe India to preserve for her, while we can, what remains of a splendid inheritance ?—*Calcutta Review, January*, 1901.

ART AND UNIVERSITY REFORM IN INDIA.

The English Board of Education in its rules for Secondary Schools, published in 1904, has defined a sound general education as that which gives a reasonable degree of exercise and development to the whole of the human faculties, without neglecting any one of them or developing one at the expense of the other. This may be accepted as a satisfactory definition of the scope of all stages of general education, and it will serve as a text in discussing from the artistic standpoint a question which, in the last few years, has aroused almost as much interest in India as the partition of Bengal—the reform of Indian Universities. Were it not that educated Europeans, especially those who have graduated in European Universities, are accustomed to regard artistic thought and culture as outside the ordinary scope of general education, it would strike most educationists that the exclusion of art from the category of human faculties is an inexplicable anomaly in the curriculum of Indian Universities. But even in Europe it is only within the last twenty or thirty years that art, as a part of general education, has been taken seriously by educationists, or advanced beyond the "drawing, stretching and fainting in coils" which excited the admiration of Alice in Wonderland and is still as popular a form of amusement in English seminaries for young ladies as it is in Indian Hill Stations.

Although art, represented primarily by a sound system of teaching drawing and design, is year by year taking a more important part in the whole scheme of national education in Europe and in America, yet the oldest of the English Universities, which for several centuries has made the study of Greek culture and civilisation the basis of its teaching, persists in ignoring the fact that one of the first principles of Greek education was the cultivation of the æsthetic faculties. Ancient Egypt stood in much the same relation to the culture of ancient Greece as ancient Greece does to the culture of our so-called classical schools. But we do not find it recorded that Hellenic youth spent any considerable part of their time in composing odes and essays in the hieroglyphic or hieratic writings, the classic Egyptian languages in which the ancient wisdom lay buried. As soon as they could read and write their own language, the young Athenians learnt by heart their own great national epics, patriotic songs and religious hymns. Afterwards, the subjects which held the highest place in their curriculum were music and drawing. The mechanical book-work and equally mechanical lecture-work with which we produce most of our school-made culture were hardly known to the art-loving and nature-loving Greek. A cultivated Greek lived and died in an atmosphere of art, an art which permeated the whole national life and every branch of learning, not founded merely on the recollection of what former generations had said, thought or done, but expressing spontaneously the thoughts, habits and aspirations of the age in which he lived.

I do not wish to argue that the ancient Greek system is entirely applicable to the needs of the present day, but I think it is important for educationists, both in India and in Europe, to remember that when ancient Greece attained to that wonderful degree of culture which they profess to take for their model, the æsthetic sense was believed to hold one of the highest places among the intellectual faculties. Nor is Greece an isolated example. History shows that the period of the highest intellectual activity in nations has nearly always coincided with, or approximated to, the period of their greatest artistic development. And the reason for this is plain, for art represents the creative and originating faculties, as distinguished from the merely receptive ones. It is only since our modern European art parted from the main-stream of the national life and drifted into the backwaters of archæology and eclecticism, that it has lost all influence on national character and culture; so that ugliness and vulgarity in the surroundings of our daily lives are looked upon with equanimity as necessary accompaniments of modern civilisation.

Japan is a striking example of the influence of a really national art upon national character and intellect; an example, moreover which approaches nearer to the Greek ideal of culture than any other in modern times —the kind of culture which English education has nearly stamped out in India. It is surely worth the attention of educationists to note that the Japanese are the most artistic nation of the present day. Like the Greek, their art is born of a feeling which has its roots deep in the national character: it is not founded merely on an unthinking imitation or reproduction of a bygone culture, like the archæological art of modern Europe, but is strongly based on the realisation of their own place in the ceaseless procession of nations.

The quality inherent in all real and honest artistic effort, which makes some form of art training especially valuable for ordinary educational purposes, is the striving to do a thing as well as it can be done, and not merely as well as circumstances permit or the exigencies of the occasion demand. That is the compelling influence in all the best art in every country and in every age. When that ceases to be its aim, and art becomes merely ostentation and vanity, it is an infallible sign of the intellectual and moral deterioration which presage national decay.

It is the true inborn artistic spirit which has taught the Japanese as a nation to make their work as perfect as hand and mind can make it, just as nature does. It is this which has contributed, in no small degree, not only to the national happiness and to the courage with which they have met every difficulty and danger, but to that intellectual receptivity and largeness which have made the Japanese people eager to adopt everything useful to them in Western institutions, while preserving intact their own national culture.

It may be said in support of the total exclusion of art from the courses of Indian Universities that they are in that respect following the precedent of similar institutions in Europe. But though the education of European Universities differs widely from the Greek ideal of culture, there will be found in the best European Universities an artistic spirit which is conspicuously wanting in the Indian ones. There is no precedent in Europe for the squalid environment, the absence of all stimulus for the spiritual side of human nature, and the neglect of all that conduces to the brightness of school or college life such as we usually find about all Indian Universities. And there is a vast difference between the whole organisation of the Indian and European University systems, one of those fundamental differences which are too often ignored when we attempt to transfer Western institutions to the East. The English school system leading up to the University is only one branch, and hardly the most important or vital branch, of national education. In India, at least in popular estimation, it stands for the whole; so that whatever is not included in the University course is generally despised by the so-called educated classes. In Europe it is only a comparatively small fraction of the educated classes that ever enters a University. In India the University courses are generally believed to embrace all forms of higher education, and the term "educated" is applied only to those who have entered, or failed to enter, a University.

It is a well-known law of nature that when a species of plant is taken from its natural environment and transplanted into a foreign soil, unless it is carefully watched, it often revenges itself upon mankind by running wild and destroying the useful plants of indigenous growth with which it comes into contact. And this is just what has happened with the educational system which India has borrowed from the West.

It has produced many plants of luxurious growth, but far too many have run to weed and crowded out the healthy, useful and beautiful plants which Indian soil has produced. The artificial culture of the West has destroyed the natural culture of the East. The want of a consistent artistic policy, which is painfully conspicuous in the whole administration of India, and the absence of all artistic considerations in the education of the youth of the country, have not only suppressed originality of thought and lowered the standard of culture, but they have brought about a state of things that neither Indian educationists nor statesmen can afford to ignore. Instead of widening the range of occupations, the present University system in India tends to narrow it. It has helped to turn the hereditary artists, of whom any country in the world might be proud, into hewers of wood and drawers of water, and driven them to swell the already overfilled ranks of competitors for Government clerkships. It has helped to bring about a depravity of public taste, even lower than the average European standard, so that the majority of Indian graduates honestly prefer the spurious and tawdry Western art for which India is the common dumping ground, to the real art of their own country. The real artists of the country, as I know from long personal experience, are often reduced to earning a miserable pittance by working for the poor and "uneducated" classes, not, as is so frequently asserted, on account of the poverty of the country, but because the rich and educated Indians for the most part waste their substance on the by-products of Western commercialism which they fondly imagine to be Western art.

I do not propose that the Universities should become a training ground for artists and art-workmen; that would neither be for the advantage of Indian art nor for the benefit of the Universities. But I do maintain that true education must recognise that the cultivation of the artistic faculties, whether it be in schools and colleges, or in the greater university of the national life (like the teaching in Japan to-day and in all European countries in former times) tends to bring out and develop all the original powers of the mind. I would argue further that the students whose instincts lead them to study nature by the methods of the artist, rather than by the methods of the man of letters or of the man of science, instead of having those instincts suppressed, as they are in the Indian University system, should be given opportunities of developing them. Indian Universities can never become worthy of the name as long as their influence encourages or compels the sons of the men who inherit all the splendid traditions of Indian art to quit their father's profession because the narrow and pedantic system of higher education leaves them neither honour nor profit in the pursuit of it.

The Calcutta University, as its late Vice-Chancellor proclaimed at the last Convocation, is the largest in the world. The population to which it professes to offer the highest of European culture and enlightenment is over one hundred millions. But from its foundation its ideal of culture has been a hybrid system of Western pedagogics, tempered by Western utilitarianism. Its influence in the past fifty years has been one of the most potent forces in hastening the ruin of national art and culture in India. It might have been expected that with the new organisation provided by Lord Curzon, it would have made some attempt to remove this reproach. The Faculty of Arts last January went so far as to accept, practically unanimously, an abstract resolution proposed by myself that "in the interests of general culture art should not be excluded from the Arts course of the University." It even accepted as an alternative for elementary science in the Matriculation Examination an equivalent instalment of artistic nature-study, such as is practised with the best results in Japanese High Schools and in some of the Colleges in Madras. But before the scheme was ratified by the Senate, it was taken out of the hands of the University and referred to a small Committee sitting at Simla. This Committee revised the draft regulations so that the new Calcutta University maintains now precisely the same attitude towards art as it did twenty years ago. That is, though it recognises law, medicine, engineering and science as fit subjects for the honours and benefits which the University bestows, it shuts out art altogether.

The new scheme, as a scheme of pedagogics, is so far an improvement on the old that it aims at and probably will achieve a much better system of teaching English literature and science. But as a scheme of national culture it presents the same obvious defects as before, namely, that it imports into India all the narrowness and exclusiveness which University teaching in Europe derived from the middle ages. It insists that the intellectual organisation of educated India must conform to one of two types, either that of the man of letters or that of the man of science. The general course of the University will afford the literary student a choice of subjects which will help him in following his particular bent; it will attract the future engineer by teaching him mechanics and higher mathematics, subjects necessary in his profession; it will assist the future medical man, or any one about to enter a scientific career, by teaching him the rudiments of science; to the lawyer who will have to plead in English law courts, it gives a sound training in English. But to the art student the University simply says—come if you will, but we do not recognise art either as one of the higher studies or as useful in the intellectual development of a University student. We have a Faculty of Arts, but the art faculty is not one we think worth cultivating.

It is not only that the hereditary artistic castes of India, which have made Indian art famous among all the nations of the earth, are thus practically shut out of all University honours and of all prospects of employment in Government service. It is not only that Schools of Art become merely refuges and asylums for those who fail in the University course. And it is not only that the exclusiveness of the system which will cram all the brains of the country into a literary or scientific mould of modern European make keeps out of the service of the state some of the best intellect of the country. It is even more destructive to national art and culture in India that the great body of students who do enter the University are deprived of any opportunity of developing the artistic sense, except through the medium of English literature. It is hard for most European educationists, trained in the narrow groove of European university teaching, to understand that the artistic sense is a faculty as important to the literary man, to the engineer, to physicians and surgeons and to advocates and judges, as it is to painters, sculptors, architects or designers. They generally regard it as an archæological formulary or a dilettante accomplishment which is easily understood and acquired by every educated man who has learnt to play with Greek iambics or become expert in modern sciences. But even if it is not so, it matters, they think, very little. Yet to educationists who realise the deep-seated defects of Indian Universities it must be clear that these very defects are largely due to the want of development of the artistic faculties in Indian teachers and students. For those who will put aside all musty educational precedents which do not affect the problem to be solved in India, and regard education as the science of training and developing all that is best and highest in human nature, and those who will clear their minds from all the shams, deceptions and false ideals which hide the true meaning and purpose of art, must acknowledge that art and education are inseparable, whatever the governing bodies of Indian Universities may say.

The essence of real culture—not the artificial culture of the modern class-room, but the real culture which is conspicuous in all the greatest epochs of human progress—lies in the development of the powers of observation and of the powers of original thought. The greatest engineer is not the man who calculates strains and stresses best, but he who shows the greatest genius in original design. Design is the foundation and root of all art. The greatest surgeons and physicians are those in whom the powers of observation are developed to the highest point. The greatest advocates and judges are those who, through the full development of all their intellectual powers, see beyond the dry technicalities of the law, and with a fine sense of proportion separate the essential from the non-essential, just as the artist—the real artist—does in his interpretation of nature.

As, therefore, the ultimate aim of every teacher must be to develop in his students the powers of observation and the powers of original thought, it cannot be to his or their advantage to discard any useful means towards that end. The means employed must be adapted, as far as possible, to the natural bent of a student's capacities, for methods which will bring out one student's latent powers, will fail to evoke any response in others. It has, however, been recognised by the best educationists, both ancient and modern, that drawing and other forms of artistic expression are admirable means of developing the powers of observation, and the practice of design is an excellent method of developing the powers of original thought. In many ways artistic design is a much more valuable and practical Educational exercise than theoretical or experimental science, which is now accepted by Indian Universities as the panacea for all the defects in the intellectual training of young India. It brings directly into play the originating faculties, whereas science teaching, unless it is of a much higher order than what is generally found in an Indian class-room, only develops the receptive powers and very easily degenerates into common cramming. It is a kind of intellectual exercise especially suitable for Indian conditions, because designing is a universal language through which all students can express their ideas freely without being hampered by the linguistic difficulties which beset them in all their other work. Only Indian college teachers can realise what an impediment to real culture is the system of making a foreign language the medium of all instruction. True art influences every vocation in life and every aspect of intellectual culture. It cannot, therefore, be reasonable or in the interest of education to keep out of the university scheme some of the most obvious, direct and practical means of artistic expression. By the policy which the reformed Calcutta University pursues, it not only disparages and depreciates the whole art of the country, but it injures the University and the cause of education in denying to the whole body of students a means of culture for which it offers no sufficient substitute. We live in an age of scientific culture, and scientific experts have now a commanding voice in the direction of higher education in India. But when the scientist has said his last word, that instinct and desire for beauty, which he himself cannot fail to observe, ignore it though he may—for it runs through the whole range of creation—will still remain the better part of human nature, just as it has ever been in all countries and in all ages. Art, in truth, is one of those greater sciences which are at the root of all science. If the artistic spirit, which is the motive power of all the higher intellectualities, human and divine, is kept out of the newly reformed Indian Universities, they will only perpetuate all the evils of the old, although Indian graduates may learn their facts better and be better instructed in natural phenomena.

The Indian Government now devotes extreme care and large sums of money to the preservation and restoration of the great monuments of Indian art. But surely, it is of more vital importance to India to keep alive the artistic spirit and to maintain the living art preserved to the present day by the descendants of the great architects and artists who created these masterpieces. As long as the Schools of Art remain altogether out of the scheme of national education, they can exercise no real influence on Indian art; and when the largest University in the world, which has for its motto "for the advancement of learning," has ordained that learning for Indian youth may be interpreted in a literary, legal, medical or scientific, but not in an artistic sense, there is little hope that anything will be done in this direction.—*East and West, January*, 1907.

of the Japanese into the front rank of modern nations to their marvellous artistic instinct. Yet a mere cursory view of history will show that the nations with the greatest artistic record have always been those whose political Empire has been the greatest and most lasting. Their rise and decay may be traced without any other documents than those their art has left in marble, stone and brick, in metal, wood and clay. Unless, therefore, we are right and all the centuries wrong, or unless the natural instinct for beauty hitherto inherent in human nature is going to be satisfactorily replaced by something else not yet manifested, it is evident that art is an index to national vitality, and cannot be left out of account by politicians whose ideas rise above a county council or the exigencies of party manœuvres.

No Anglo-Indian statesman has fully understood the administrative uses of art. Akbar, whose rule presents many analogies to our own, showed his marvellous political genius more conspicuously in his understanding of art than in the organisation of the machinery by which he collected his revenues, or in his measures for securing justice and social order. Wherever the monuments of Akbar's reign exist, Hindu, Jain, Buddhist and Muhammadan alike testify to the gladness and contentment which his benevolent despotism

INDIAN ADMINISTRATION & 'SWADESHI.'

A few years ago in an article in the "Indian Review,"* on the masterpiece of Mogul art, the Taj at Agra, I ventured to draw attention to the importance, from an imperial point of view, of Englishmen studying and trying to understand the artistic ideals of the East, for, I said, the Indian Question, which then seemed smaller than a man's hand, might fill the Eastern horizon to-morrow. I may, perhaps, without posing as a prophet, quote this as an example of how in the East the unexpected is always happening, for to-day Indian and Eastern questions loom in our political sky as large as Home Rule for Ireland—which to stay-at-home politicians, who make no attempt to grasp the significance of Eastern problems, may seem a monstrously overdrawn comparison.

To many others whose education and environment have taught them to regard art as external to the serious affairs of life, and only a pleasant amusement for hours of leisure, it may not be easy to understand the connection between art and politics, or to trace the coming

---

*'The Taj and Its Designers,' June, 1903.

brought to the people. In this record of national art those who have eyes to see can see that Akbar achieved—what so far we have not succeeded in winning—a sincere understanding between the rulers and the ruled, a sentiment deeper than respect or astonishment. It is just that note of gladness which we have failed to evoke. We bring with us into India the dull, grey northern skies, and in spite of all that we have done we are still looked upon by most Indians as stern and strict schoolmasters, rather than as friends and fellow-citizens of the Empire. This comes chiefly from our failure to grasp the fundamental fact that art is a far more important matter of State policy in India than it is in Europe—just because in India art is still the voice of the people. To be out of touch with a people's art is to be out of touch with the people.

The discipline which we have imposed upon India has been—at least for the time being—a great blessing, but the dulness is not an essential part of the discipline. Our Indian Empire is now held by a departmental machinery so immense and so complex that no administrator in modern times has been able to do what Akbar did. Lord Curzon attempted it and might have succeeded, were it not that by the peculiar system through which we govern our Indian Empire India is deprived of his services just when his work was beginning. His wonderful energy and intellectual powers have done much to improve the machinery, but that welding of the administrative system on to the national life, which Akbar achieved and which we must achieve before we can regard India as an integral part of the British Empire, has still to be done. Lord Curzon, moreover, is, unfortunately for India, an ardent archæologist. I say this without disrespect and without the least intention of depreciating the splendid work which he has done in restoring Indian monuments. It was a work to which Lord Curzon devoted the best of his great intellect and artistic sympathy, and no artist can have other than the most sincere admiration for the results. But in seven years Lord Curzon had not time to realise what no Anglo-Indian administrator has yet learnt in a life time—that in India art is not archæology. What Lord Curzon failed to do in seven years his successors can hardly hope to do in five; so, although the Taj, the palaces of the Moguls, and many other splendid monuments of India's past bear the mark of Lord Curzon's great personality, Indian art remains where it was—on the road to ruin—unless 'Swadeshi' should come to the rescue.

It says much for the thoroughness and enthusiasm with which Lord Curzon did his work that at the end of his seven years' labours he succeeded in digging through the surface layers on which most of our Indian administrative system is built, and struck against the bed-rock of what we may call Indian nationality, though that word fails to express exactly what Swadeshi is. It may be that he did so unconsciously, but, nevertheless, if through his action he has prepared the way for a more solid and enduring foundation on which the administrative fabric may be built, Lord Curzon deserves well of the Empire.

In discussing Swadeshi it is necessary to distinguish between the true Swadeshi and the false, and it may be said at once that Manchester can laugh at the false one, and need not fear the true, for a happy and prosperous India is Manchester's best friend. India has need of the method of Manchester as well as the artistic sense of Swadeshi. The false Swadeshi is just now the most conspicuous, for it is noisy and self-assertive. It preaches thinly-veiled sedition and talks largely of patriotism, though it is as absurd to talk of patriots of India as it would be to talk of patriots of Europe. It will help a decaying national industry when it can be used as a political lever, but will leave it to starve and die out when it does not serve that purpose. Its methods are generally hollow, unpractical and insincere; but though it justly deserves our contempt we should never forget that it is largely the product of our own educational system.

The true Swadeshi keeps aloof from the official administration, and neither joins in the scramble for official favours nor apes the noisy manner of the Western demagogue. It lives its own life apart from ours, and many Anglo-Indians spend a lifetime in India hardly conscious of its existence. You may see its various outward manifestations on the ghats at Benares, and learn that though there are many formularies—Hindu, Sikh, Jain, Buddhist and Muhammadan—it has one ideal. That ideal is so different from ours that few Europeans attempt to understand it, and few would succeed in less than a cycle of transmigrations. It is something more than nationality. It is the Eastern way of thinking. This Swadeshi is not disloyal, though it has its sinister aspect, which it revealed in 1857. It is not for us; but it is grateful for the *pax Britannica*, and realises its value. It bides it time; it has faith in the centuries—*and unless all Indian history lies, the centuries are on its side.*

It is this Swadeshi which, from the time the Aryans entered into India, has absorbed one conquering race after another without materially altering its way of thinking. It is an immense political force, now passive on the whole, but getting more active every day, for its strength, which was dissipated by a long period of anarchy and misrule, is being slowly recruited under our firm and stable government. We, to a certain extent, like Akbar, found our Indian system of revenue, law and police upon it, but in many vital matters in which art is concerned, such as industrial development, public works, and national education, we almost completely ignore it. It is in the matter of industrial development that Swadeshi has lately shown a remarkable activity and drawn European attention to the fact of its existence. How little our Anglo-Indian departmentalism has been aware of this side of Swadeshi is shown by the fact that until a few years ago official statistics referred to Anglo-Indian cotton mills, which give employment to only 350,000 people, as representing the most important industry in India after agriculture. Not long ago an official, considered a high authority on industrial matters, lectured to an Anglo-Indian audience in London and described the handweaving industry of India as almost driven out of the market—the fact being that it still supports directly and indirectly, not thousands, but millions of Indian villagers. The hand industry is not only of far greater importance than the whole of the steam-power factories put together, but contributes largely towards their support by purchasing the greater part of the yarn which the Indian steam mills produce.

The concentration of labour and machinery rendered necessary by the use of steam power, the struggle of the agricultural labourer for 'bettering' himself, and of the capitalist to add to his capital, have given Lancashire its steam mills in which, according to a competent authority, the weaving industry is carried on under conditions unhealthy and dangerous, bad for mind and body, making women unfit for motherhood, cursing the children and causing the people to deteriorate. The remarkable development of hand-loom weaving in the last twenty years does not support the popular belief that the power loom will drive out the hand loom altogether even in Europe. In India, after 150 years of fighting with obsolete weapons against all the resources of European mechanical science, the almost forgotten hand-loom industry is still a highly organised and very formidable industrial army. This is because in the first place heredity makes the Indian caste weaver a highly skilled artisan, and secondly, because his Swadeshi way of thinking does not give the Indian labourer that passion for mere money-making which the West calls laudable ambition. The Indian people, the true Swadeshi, are at heart philosophical and deeply religious. Every peasant believes that if he is faithful to his *dharma* (his duty to God and the State) in this life, his *karma* (his place in the cosmos) may make him a king in the next re-birth. Why then should he struggle for mere wealth in this? So the high wages of modern industrialism—which in Europe draw the life-blood of nations to the great cities—in India attract only the scum of the population. Only when starvation drives him to the famine-camp or to the cities will the peasant leave his plough and the skilled weaver his loom.

The agitation against the partition of Bengal has brought to the aid of the Indian hand-loom weaver all the forces of Swadeshi, both the real and the sham, and bids fair to solve in a twelvemonth a problem which has puzzled departmentalism for fifty years—technical education for India. The despised occupation of weaving has become one which attracts the intelligence of the highest castes. The best appliances of modern Europe are being brought to replace the primitive apparatus of the village hand-loom weaver, who suddenly finds himself in great demand as a teacher for Brahmins and Vaishyas and for "failed B.A's" of the Calcutta University. One of Lord Curzon's last acts was to sanction for Bengal an important scheme for a school of hand-loom weaving on the best modern lines, which will help to turn many noisy agitators into loyal and industrious citizens. The Indian weaving industry will thus be able to face the competition of nineteenth century factories on more equal terms. The latest improvements in the application of mechanical power all tend to make the concentration of labour in these social pest-houses less and less a necessity for modern industrial methods. It is more than probable that before many decades have passed modern science will place at the disposal of the Indian village weaver, in a simple and effective form, as much power as he may want to use. Thus the centuries even now are helping Swadeshi.

Let us now discuss Swadeshi in relation to public works. For the last fifty years departmentalism has entrusted the whole art interests of India to a body of engineers who have had no artistic training. I say 'whole art interests' advisedly, for if all the Schools of Art in India were closed to-morrow Indian art would be hardly a wit the worse—or better. Art museums as they have been always conducted may give a spasmodic impulse to a passing caprice of fashion in Europe and America, by advertising so-called Indian art ware. But, unfortunately, most of the art collected in Indian museums and exhibitions is made solely for the European market. It is an art which from its falseness can never have a permanent commercial value, and it is not in any sense the art of the people. A permanent revival of Indian art, either in a commercial or artistic sense, can never be produced by such methods as these.

The monopoly of architectural art which the Indian Public Works Department has assumed, and the curse of a false classicism which it has brought with it from Europe, are the principal causes of the decay of the real art of the country. The complacency with which Anglo-Indian administrators have regarded the ineptitude of this policy is partly, no doubt, a recognition of the splendid and devoted services of Public Works officers in the construction of railways and irrigation works, but it is mainly due to the ineradicable superstition that European architecture is better adapted for modern requirements, and that though Indian architects may have excelled in the aesthetic side of their profession, they are far behind the times in all that relates to constructional science. We form our ideas of Indian art from the precious inlay of the Taj or from the exuberant carving of Jain and Hindu temples. But do we generally take the mosaic of St. Mark's at Venice as the criterion of the cost of a post-office, or form the estimates of a hospital on the carving of a Gothic cathedral? Indian architects, like those of mediæval Europe, know how to be economical when economy is wanted, though they disregard economy when it is neither becoming nor necessary. In other words they are trained in all the requirements of their profession.

It is doubtless true that Indian builders of the present day know little of the use of iron for building purposes, but it is important to remember that brick, stone, and wood have not yet been entirely superseded as building materials in India, either by iron, glass, *papiermaché*, sawdust or any other of the up-to-date resources of Western architects. In the purely constructional use of these old-fashioned meterials all that European builders have achieved, whether in classic, mediæval, or modern times, has been equalled or excelled by Indian architects; and it is highly probable that if Anglo-Indian engineers had attempted to study and make use of the traditional craftmanship of centuries which the descendants of these men keep alive, they would have learnt something of the artistic possibilities of iron girders, for the native builders, instinctively, will use corrugated iron and kerosene tins more artistically than we do.

We pride ourselves on being a practical nation, and the popular excuse for any act of vandalism, or any peculiarly stupid artistic abomination, is that art must give way to considerations of utility. Yet when art becomes a question of public policy, we are probably the most unpractical and irrational of all civilised nations. We have certainly exhibited ourselves in the light in India, both before and since Great Britain assumed imperial responsibility for the government of the country. Some time ago I met in Calcutta a Prussian State engineer, sent out officially to India by his Government to study the constructive principles of Indian architecture. Our Teutonic friends are more practical than ourselves. It was an English chemist who discovered aniline dyes. The Germans forthwith appropriated the discovery, and built up a gigantic German industry upon it. Now they are rapidly taking from us the Indian indigo trade. Englishmen opened the door to Sanscrit literature, but German scholars placed the study of it on a scientific basis, and when we want Principals for the few Indian colleges where Oriental literature is a special study, we must generally send to Germany for them. A Scotchman, James Fergusson, spent forty years of his life in exploring the marvellous field of architectural research, scientific and artistic, which our Indian Empire affords. His labours have been lost on Indian departmentalism, and it seems likely that the Germans again will be the first Europenn nation to profit by his life-work.

Indian departmentalism consistently shuts its eyes to the fact that India still has a national art. England had one—two centuries ago, and is now seriously attempting to revive it, but the national culture which was the product of centuries cannot be restored in a day. Mr. Edward S. Prior, in a monograph on the Cathedral Builders of England, * which should be a text-book for all who wish to understand Indian art, has described the process by which the classicism of the Italian Renaissance and that peculiar product of modern times, archæological art, have destroyed the traditional, national art of Europe, just in the same way as the national art of India is now being destroyed by departmentalism. He has shown how in every country and every epoch before the eighteenth century a national architecture was created by trained bodies of craftsmen, organised like the artisan caste of India, so that every building was a school of painting, sculpture and engineering—of art and of craft; every cathedral, church, palace, or mansion, a human document in which was written the life of the nation; every public building in its stability, durability, and beauty, a symbol of the power and dignity of the State. Then came that era of paper architects, of archæologists and rabid commercialism. So instead of a national art

* *The Port folio* No. 46, November, 1905.

which was a joyous worship of the Creator in the daily work of the people—for the cottager as well as for the King —we have now an art for 'best parlours' and 'at homes'; an art for museums and exhibitions; an art for the scholar, too absorbed in the dust-heaps of the past to concern himself with the beauty of the present; an art for the merchant, too busy with his money-bags to worship God on week-days.

In India we have now an exactly similar process leading to exactly similar results, only carried on with greater ruthlessness and less artistic understanding, for we have in India no Christopher Wren or Inigo Jones to give us brilliant essays in archæological architecture. India still possesses a large body of trained craftsmen who practise the art of building on similar principles and producing similar results as the great mediæval builders of Europe. They enter no University, for Indian Universities were founded for supplying material for the official machinery, and make no provision either for art or religion. But their ancestors built the Taj, the shrines of Mount Abu, and countless other masterpieces; they constructed the Mogul palaces, public offices, irrigation works, and everything of practical utility that the art of building could provide.

How does our departmentalism provide for these needs to-day? A certain number of young men, with no training either in art or in craft, learn by heart certain formularies of calculating the maximum weight which an iron girder will bear, the smallest dimensions to which a wall can be reduced without collapsing, the cheapest rate at which a building can be constructed so as to bring it within the annual departmental budget. When a department has settled on paper the plan of the building it wants, one of these engineers with an archæological turn of mind puts on to it a 'Gothic' or 'classic' front, according to departmental taste, and provides a certain scale of departmental decoration according to departmental rank and dignity. Then the hereditary Indian craftsman whose family has practised the art of building for untold centuries is brought in to learn the wisdom of the West by copying the departmental paper patterns. How bad the art becomes is, perhaps, difficult to be understood by those to whom an archæological solecism is more offensive than an artistic eyesore; but it is easy to explain how wasteful and extravagant the system really is. To build one of the latest and perhaps the best of these archæological structures in Calcutta, a large number of Indian caste-builders were employed. Many of them were both artists and crafts-men—they could design, build, and carve. The structural design had been settled for them departmentally, so they had no concern with that. There was also a considerable amount of ornament to be carved, but that also had been designed for them in proper departmental style, which happened to be Italian Renaissance, so they were not allowed to attempt that. Other men, who had been trained in the European archælogical style in Bombay were brought over to copy mechanically the paper patterns prepared for them. These men were paid two rupees a day each. Now there are at the present time in the Orissa district, not far from Calcutta, and famous for its splendid native architecture, a considerable number of masons and builders who, within the last twenty years, have designed and carried out architectural decoration comparable with that of our finest mediæval buildings in Europe, and infinitely more beautiful than the imitation Renaissance ornament of the building I have referred to. The average earnings of these men is four annas a day, or one-eighth of the wages paid for executing the departmental decoration. They and their fellow-artists all over India are constantly in want of work, for departmentalism has no need of their services. Indian art cries out for bread; we give it museums, exhibitions, and archæology.

The departmental plea of economy will not bear a moment's careful examination. Departmental economy at best is the economy of the limited liability company which keeps up an appearance of prosperity by paying dividends out of capital; for the imitation of a dead classicism which we hold up to the natives of India as the best product of Western civilisation is sapping the foundations of Indian art in the same way as it has destroyed the national art of Europe. In so doing we recklessly use up a part of the resources of our Indian Empire, infinitely more valuable than all its gold mines or coal mines—resources which, properly utilised, might bring to the revenues of the country as much as any department of the State. Anglo-Indian architectural works are rarely even relatively economical; for the native builders under our inartistic system are rapidly losing the sentiment of good craftsmanship, which always accompanies the artistic sentiment. In the same way the decay of national sentiment in European art has produced the modern school of jerry-builders. The process of alterations, patchwork, and repairs which Indian public buildings now require, is not entered against the capital account, so that does not trouble the departmental budgets. But when Macaulay's New Zealander, who in some far-off time will continue the *dilettante* propensities of our race, turns his attention from the ruins of London to the sites of great Anglo-

Indian cities, he will sketch and wonder what rude barbarians left mud-heaps for memorials among the stately relics of native imperial rule. Swadeshi builds for posterity—we for ourselves. Are we right and all the centuries wrong?

The third vital matter of Indian administration which I have mentioned above is national education. From this, Indian Universities, like their European models, are unanimous in excluding art. It is a common saying that an artist who wishes to know his faults should give his work to be copied by his pupils. Indian Universities, with the unerring short-sightedness of the copyist, have exaggerated the defects of the older English Universities to the point of caricature. The many excellencies of English college-culture are too well advertised by its votaries to need mention. Indian Universities have only recognised its faults—the aloofness from the national life and want of breadth. Inversely, Oxford has attempted to reproduce Greek culture by composing Greek odes and essays—ignoring the fact that it was based on the cultivation of the æsthetic faculties and a profound study of human nature—while Japan has caught the true spirit of it in not attempting an imitation.

Lord Curzon has given Indian Universities a new machinery. They have now to work out their own salvation with it, and are apparently about to restore Indian culture on a basis of modern science. The idea that teaching Indian schoolboys a smattering of modern experimental science will be a revelation to a culture and civilisation which constructed a theory of the Universe, based on what we call modern scientific principles five thousand years ago, must make Swadeshi laugh in its sleeves; but the difficulty of applying Western ideas to the East is shown even in metaphors —for Swadeshi generally has no sleeves. The Greeks believed that, by teaching their children to love God's beauty in Nature, they would help them to bring beauty into their daily lives. They thus found what modern educationists are always looking for—a religion without dogma. Every national art since the world began expresses the same sentiment. In Europe we still believe in beauty to a certain extent provided that it is archæologically correct. In India we only believe in unadulterated ugliness and moral text-books. The Greeks understood that, by the study of nature and of art, they were developing the powers of observation and the powers of original thought, as art represents the creative faculties developed through the observation of nature. Greek education was, therefore, a system of national culture based on national life and art. The present Indian University system is a system of pedagogics based on narrow utilitarianism.

The artistic sense is the essence of real culture. Homer, Shakespeare, and the Mahabharata, products of national life and art, will live when most of our college-made culture is lost in the limbo of time. But art, as the vitalising influence in national culture, is as little understood by Indian Universities as it is by departmentalism. The art faculty only exists as part of the University machinery. Swadeshi in Bengal has raised a cry for a national University. Though there may be sedition in the cry, there is none in the idea itself; it is the ideal for which all Indian educationists must aim. A real national University would solve the greatest difficulty of Indian education—the question of religion. However suitable it may be for the Western social and political system to exclude religion from State education, the idea is, and always will be, utterly incomprehensible and abhorrent to the East. By transplanting this system to India we make Indian colleges hot-beds of irreligion and disloyalty, and only create a Frankenstein to curse and hate us. Akbar solved the difficulty by inventing a religion for the State, and at the same time allowing all his subjects to practise theirs. We could do the same by founding a Christian University and giving State aid to all other creeds in founding their own. Swadeshi would then be wholly on our side. We should hoist sedition with its own petard and convert an armed camp into a loyal and contented Empire.

It may be that art is merely a matter of sentiment; but sentiment has brought Japan where she is to-day, and if the centuries can be trusted, sentiment rules the world. The bigotry of Aurangzebe destroyed the art of the Moguls and broke up the empire which the sword of Babar and the statesmanship of Akbar founded. Is there not a danger to the Empire which Warren Hastings, Clive, Wellesley, and Dalhousie won for us in the short-sighted departmentalism which crushes out the spirituality of the people? That is not the white man's mission.—*Nineteenth Century and After, June,* 1907.

THE USES OF ART.

[Lecture given on the Anniversary meeting of the Chaitanya Library, Calcutta, December, 1905.]

Perhaps one of the greatest difficulties which artists and art teachers meet with in the present day arises from the popular view of art as something separate from, if not altogether opposed to, practical use. Any student of art will soon realise that this is entirely contrary to all the teaching of art tradition and history, but nevertheless it is one which has a firm hold upon public opinion; especially in Europe where within the last two centuries the old artistic traditions have been superseded by a new order of things, which has not yet had time to adjust itself to national needs.

In India, too, under the British administration this idea has taken firm root, and its influence is conspicuous in most of the institutions, educational and administrative, which India has borrowed from Europe. Indian Universities, faithfully imitating their European models, exclude art from their curriculum, treating it as a non-essential factor in national culture. The place of the Indian architects—whose forefathers, it must be remembered, built not only the Taj, the exquisite palaces of the Moguls and splendid shrines of religion, but great irrigation works, bridges and public buildings—is everywhere being filled by engineers whose practical knowledge is supposed to more than compensate for the want of artistic training. Indian art has come to be regarded either as a beautiful relic of antiquity for which no place can be found in modern life, or as a curiosity made chiefly for the delectation of our cold-weather visitors from Europe.

Particularly in Bengal, where we nearly always import our art ready-made from Europe, or manufacture it locally from European patterns, it plays a very small part, both in private and in public affairs. It is one of these superfluities which we never consider essential either for our spiritual or material well-being; but when it does come into our life, it is only when we have satisfied what we are pleased to consider our practical requirements. In other words, art is regarded as something essentially ornamental, rather than useful.

If it be true that art has really, in the present day, entered upon a new phase in which it ceases to play an essential part in our national life, it must inevitably follow that art, as we take it, must sooner or later cease to exist; for there is no natural law more sure in its working than the one which ordains the extinction of everything which no longer serves its intended use in the cosmos. A muscle in our bodies which is never exercised soon becomes atrophied and incapable of use. Creatures which are deprived of light soon become blind. An intellectual faculty which is never exerted is soon deprived of the power of exertion. Modern science is sometimes inclined to boast of its power of controlling nature, but we must never forget that we only control nature through natural laws and cannot infringe them in the smallest degree without suffering the penalties which nature imposes. The laws of art, like most others that regulate human affairs, are founded upon nature's laws.

In considering, therefore, the proper relation of art to the necessities of human life it is better to go straight to nature and study the principles we find there, rather than to rely only upon the precedents of history. And if there is one principle which is more conspicuous than another throughout the whole domain of nature, it is the intimate association of beauty with use. The desire for beauty shows itself in the whole order of the universe, from the tiniest atom in the earth under our feet, to the magnificent phenomena of the sky and atmosphere above and around us. Man as the highest product of creation, asserts the right of considering himself at once the most beautiful and the most useful, and I am not going to say anything in dispute of that claim. But you will find the same principle manifesting itself in endless variations in the beasts, birds, fishes and insects and in every living thing; in every leaf and flower that grows, and, further down in the scale, in metals, rocks and stones, and even in things animate and inanimate too minute for the unaided eye to see.

And as you examine this universal principle more closely you will never find that the beauty is something apart from usefulness, a thing which can be substracted or left out. In nature beauty and usefulness are inseparable. It is only in man's crude and imperfect work that usefulness is so often associated with ugliness. Art in nature is the joy of the Creator in perfecting His handiwork. Art in man's work is but the faint echo of the divine on earth repeating the joy of the Creator. Art, then, is in a special sense a form of worship, and you will observe that the finest art in all countries has nearly always been produced in the service of religion. But whether the art was applied to religious purposes, to works of public utility or to common domestic needs, you will find one spirit in all good art in all countries and in all epochs—the same spirit as you see in nature's work—the striving to make the work fit for the purpose for which it was intended. Art, in the abstract, thus becomes the striving to do things well. There is no question of separating utility and beauty—the joy of perfecting the use, consciously or unconsciously, creates the beauty.

Some will perhaps argue that the ugliness generally conspicuous in modern engineering works, railways, bridges, motor-cars and other things undeniably useful, is a proof that use and beauty are often incompatible. But I maintain that the ugliness of these things is not a necessity, but only conclusive evidence of their imperfection. You must remember that the application of iron to building purposes and its use in relation to steam and electric power are but things of yesterday. The beautiful forms which art has created in olden times from the use of brick, stone, wood, and other materials were slowly evolved in thousands of years by the experience and practice of hundreds of generations of craftsmen. There is every reason, therefore, to believe that as our engineers gain more experience and skill in the use of new materials, and in the manifold applications of the new forces now brought into the service of mankind, they will gradually produce more and more beautiful forms and learn the lesson which nature teaches—perfect fitness is perfect beauty. In fact, the finest works of modern engineering are by no means without a beauty of their own.

But you may ask, is there not art for art's sake, beauty for beauty's sake? Yes, surely there is, just as there is mind and body, spirit and matter. Yet, as Emerson says, as soon as beauty is sought after, not for religion and love, but for pleasure, it degrades the seeker. The motive of the artist is writ large in every work of his hand and brain. If the motive is base, the art will be tainted with that baseness. Why is it that so much of our modern painting and sculpture is small and petty compared with even the average productions of ancient Greece, the works of medieval times, or of the sixteenth century? It is because the artists of the past employed their genius in the service of religion and of the state. They worked for God and for humanity. Our modern art is mostly for private vanity and amusement. Pictures and statues are goods and chatels to be bought and sold. The man in the street thinks he is entitled to get the art he wants merely because he pays for it, and the artist is more often anxious to gratify the man who pays than to consider what he owes to art and to himself. No longer intimately associated with the service of church and state, art has become a society toy and a mere item of merchandise in the catalogues of modern commerce. The common trade expressions of art-furniture, art-wood-work, art-metal-work, reflect the popular sentiment towards all art. Plain, ordinary furniture and metal-work, such as an honest workman will produce without any pretence at being artistic, are believed to be necessarily ugly. If you want to be fashionably artistic you must pay something extra and call in the artist, who will make your things beautiful, but you must be prepared to sacrifice something of utility.

In former days in Europe trade was to a very large extent controlled by artists, through the great art-guilds, and the craftsman and the artist were one and the same person ; or at least the artist was always one who had served a thorough apprenticeship in his craft—just as your Indian artists generally are even in the present day. Leonardo da Vinci, one of the greatest artists Europe ever produced, was the greatest engineer of his time. Refaelle and Michelangelo, and many of the great masters of the Renaissance, designed the buildings for which their paintings and sculpture were intended ; and the men who built them were only inferior artists to themselves. In modern European buildings the architect is often only a draftsman who for want of architectural knowledge imitates the design of some ancient buildings intended for totally different purposes, the builder is a contractor who employs men to copy mechanically the architect's archæological essays : his first aim is to make as much profit as he can, and his art consists in putting bad ornament to conceal the faults of the design and construction.

The general inferiority of modern art thus merely reflects the narrowness of the utilitarianism and commercialism of the present age. Art, in all countries, always reflects the varying phases of national sentiment. You may trace a nation's intellectual and moral progress, or decay, much more clearly and convincingly through its art than through its written history; for art is a record which seldom lies. A vigorous and healthy national art connotes a vigorous and healthy nation. The nations with the greatest art have always been the leaders in the world's progress. Japan, which has suddenly sprung to the front rank of nations, is the most artistic nation of the present day. I venture to think that if the younger students who make use of the Chaitanya Library devoted more time to the study of art and art history they would gain a clearer insight into the moral, intellectual, and material growth of nations than they get now from their University text-books.

The present University system entirely excludes art from its scope, and this, I venture to say, is one of the principal reasons why, as a scheme of national culture, it has completely failed to satisfy India's needs. The vitalising influence in true national culture is the artistic sense, and there must be something fundamentally unsound in the University system which leads the educated classes to prefer tawdry commercialism, which generally represents European art in India, to the real art of their own country, and, instead of broadening the basis of culture drives the artists of the country to seek employment in office clerkships.

A system of education which excludes both art and religion can never succeed because it shuts out the two great influences which mould the national character. There are obvious difficulties in a state-aided University identifying itself with religious teaching, but art is neutral ground upon which all creeds and schools of thought can meet. Until educationists in India recognise that the artistic sense is as necessary in the training of men of letters, of scientists, and of engineers, as it is in that of artists, no reforms in mere methods of teaching or examination systems will place higher education on the right road.

When Greece was conquered by Rome, Greek art and Greek culture were transplanted to Italy, where they grew and flourished exceedingly for many centuries afterwards. When the Moguls conquered Hindustan Indian art commenced one of its most glorious epochs. Why is it that in spite of our honest endeavours to improve Indian art we have only succeeded in bringing bad European art to India and bad Indian art to Europe? You will find the answer in those two wonderful ruined cities of Italy and Northern India—Pompei and Fatehpur Sikri. In Pompei you will see Greek art in the forum, in the streets, in the shops, in the frescoes on the walls of the villas, in the furniture, and even in the cooking pots which are left in the fireplaces. At Fatehpur Sikri you will see Indian art in Akbar's palace, in his office, in his baths and in his stables, in all the public buildings and in the houses of his nobles. Everywhere in Pompei and in Fatehpur Sikri you will find art brought into practical use.

It was a great misfortune for Indian art that at the time when European institutions began to be introduced into India all the old artistic traditions of Europe had been swept away by the social and industrial revolution, which began in the eighteenth century, and that the art of building had come to mean only the art of applying certain rigid archæological formulæ called "styles" to the superficial embellishment of the construction. If Europe could have sent to India a practical tradition of art, as it was practised in Europe down to the eighteenth century, Indian art would not have suffered but would have gained immensely by the stimulus of fresh ideas and varied experiences just as Greek art was stimulated in the days of the Roman Empire and Indian art in the time of the Moguls. But Europe has now no living artistic traditions to offer you. We have only the feeble imitation of extinct styles, or the painful efforts of individualists struggling to work out, each one for himself, a new foundation for art to rest upon. In India you have in your living traditional art a sure and solid foundation, the only one on which art has really flourished in any country.

Within the last fifty years, there has been in England and in many countries in Europe, a remarkable development of art which has to some extent revived the artistic sense of the people, and brought about at least a partial return to those methods and principles without which no real art can exist. But from this great movement art in India has as yet received no benefit, and Indian art continues to decay, because it is regarded by Europeans, and by most Indians with European education, as made for nothing but curiosities. Let us therefore examine more closely the popular theory which has done, and is still doing, so much harm to art in India, that Indian art is no longer of practical use.

Akbar, one of the greatest and most far-seeing of Indian statesmen fully recognised the political uses of art. You cannot expect to guage the profounder depths of a people's sentiments if you do not understand their art. This wonderful artistic sympathy and understanding were inherited by his son and grandson—Jahangir and Shah Jahan—with Aurangzib, who had neither artistic sympathy nor understanding, began the decline of the Mogul Empire. I will not however, pursue this point further. I would only observe that one of the most distinguished of English politicians the other day remarked that if he and his friends, who call themselves Unionist Free-Traders, found there was no standing room between the existing political parties, they would give up politics altogether and devote themselves to art and literature. This is one of the uses of art which is open to politicians of all parties. I would especially commend it to the schoolboy politicians of Bengal.

One of the most important of the civic and domestic uses of art in all countries is to provide houses for the people to live in, and public buildings in which to conduct the affairs of state. From the latter of these uses Indian art has been almost completely excluded in modern times, and Indian builders have been taught to imitate the modern eclectic styles of Europe in the belief that these only are suitable for modern practical requirements. It would be most extraordinary if the hereditary builders of India, who for untold centuries have kept alive the traditions of their art, and adapted them time after time to the changes of fashion which one conquering race after another has brought into India, should now be found really incapable of meeting the very elementary practical requirements of modern public and private buildings. I venture to say that there is not a single modern building in India, the construction of which presents engineering difficulties at all to be compared with those which have been successfully met by Indian builders in former times.

Stability and durability are surely essentials of a practical kind in public buildings, places of worship, and other architectural works of a governing race which has faith in the greatness of its mission and in the permanence of its rule. In these respects it can hardly be disputed that Indian builders who have been true to their old traditions have always worked on sounder principles than those which have been observed in modern Indian architecture. The great monuments of Hindu and Mahomedan rule all over India which have stood for centuries exposed to all the fierce destructive influences of the Indian climate, the iconoclasm of invaders and the vandalism of philistines are incontrovertible evidence of the fact.

Fergusson, the greatest authority on Indian architecture, ancient and modern, gives an instance of the constructive skill and fine workmanship of Indian builders directed by their own architects. The terraced roof of the great mosque at Kalburgah, one of the finest monuments of Pathan rule in the Deccan, covering an area of 33,000 square feet, was in his time in seemingly good repair after four centuries of comparative neglect, although any crack or settlement would have been fatal to the whole building. I think it would be difficult to find large modern public buildings in India without cracks or leaks, and most of them would be in ruins before many years of the neglect to which the majority of Indian buildings have been exposed for centuries. In the more difficult problems of roof-construction, Indian architects have far surpassed all Europeans. The Bijapur architects invented the ingenious and beautiful method of balancing the weight of a dome inside the building instead of the more clumsy and ugly expedient of throwing it outside. The most remarkable example of this, the dome of the tomb of Mahmud at Bijapur is larger than the famous masterpiece of Roman architecture, the Pantheon at Rome. Fergusson has described it as a wonder of constructive skill. The same authority in speaking of one of the finest churches in London by the great English architect Sir Christopher Wren says:—" It would have been greatly improved had its resemblance to a Hindu porch been more complete. The necessity of confining the dome within four walls greatly injures the effect compared with the Indian examples. Even the Indian plan of roofing might be used in such a building with much less expense and constructive danger than in a Gothic vault of the same extent."

The descendants of the architects who showed such remarkable constructive invention and skill still practise their art in Rajputana, the Punjab and the United Provinces, and are only prevented from rivalling the great achievements of their ancestors because they are allowed no opportunity of doing so, except in a few of the native states in which the blind imitation of debased European art has not yet become fashionable. Fergusson admitted that he had learnt more from these men of the principles of architecture as practised by the great architects of medieval Europe than he had gained from all the books he had read. Yet these are the men who are ignored by Indian Universities, excluded from the system of Public Works and neglected by their own countrymen, because they are supposed to be deficient in practical knowledge.

It will not be necessary to quote more instances of the kind if you will only reflect that a living national art is always essentially a common sense art, because it is created by popular needs and adapted to the country which produces it. You would then realise the wrong you do to Indian art and to yourselves by following imported fashions, which even if they truly represented the best European culture and civilisation, can never be really suited to your requirements. These fashions do not, in fact, represent the best that Europe can produce, but only an effete and corrupt classicism now gradually being superseded by stronger and healthier art impulses.

The architecture which India is substituting for its own living styles is the very negation of practical common sense. It is what Fergusson calls "an art which is not conducted on truthful or constructive principles, but on imitative attempts to produce something which has no affinity with the building in hand—an art whose utterances, whether classic or Gothic, are the products of the leisure of single minds, not always of the highest class;" while your own living Indian art is "the result of the earnest thinking of thousands of minds spread over hundreds years, and acting in unison with the national voice which called it into existence."

If there are any students of engineering among the members of this society, I would advise them that they will become better engineers the more they study art, and especially the more they study the art shown in Indian architecture. But let their art be in their engineering and not something outside of it. Most of modern buildings in India would be better if they were divested of the ornament which has been applied in the belief that art begins and ends with ornament. I would ask them above all to remember Fergusson's dictum that architecture is not archæology. Certainly it is a great thing that all Indians should learn to love and venerate the great monuments of their forefathers, but it is of greater—far greater—moment that they should strive to hand on to their children those traditions which bring into the living present India's history, her culture and her art.

Greatly, as I venerate the splendid achievements of Indian art in bygone days, I would see without a pang the Taj, the palaces of the Moguls and the other great relics of antiquity, crumbling into dust, if by their ruin India could be brought to realise the priceless value of the true living art which is part of India's spiritual heritage from her glorious past.

I will pass over another of the important uses of art, that of providing clothes for the people to wear, because, in the first place, it is a subject on which my views are already very well known, and secondly, because, though from an artistic point of view it is most desirable that you should retain your own artistic dress, it is of much more importance that you should learn to live and think artistically. Eleven years ago Sir Alexander Miller, formerly legal member of the Viceroy's Council, in addressing this society on Representative Government, reminded you that in the endeavour to reach the blessings of good government national character is of infinitely greater importance than any institutions, representative or otherwise. The most important of the uses of art, of the real living art, is its influence on national character. You will see it in the character of that great nation, the Japanese. What do you think inspired the magnanimity, humanity, devotion and self-control which they have shown in this great crisis of their history, but the innate and supreme artistic sense of the people?

I will give you an instance of the same true artistic spirit which may be found also in India at the present day. Not so far from Calcutta, at Jajpur, the ancient capital of Orissa, the splendid art of stone-carving which flourished there in former days still lingers in obscurity. For the last 20 or 30 years a few of your real Indian artists have been devotedly working on a pittance of four annas a day carving decoration, more beautiful than any to be found in this city of palaces, for the temple of Biroja in that town. Their wages are paid by a *sadhu*, a religious mendicant, who has spent his whole life in begging for funds for this purpose. That is the spirit in which all true art is produced. It is the spirit with which the glorious Gothic cathedrals of mediæval Europe were built. It is the moving spirit in everything great and noble that ever art creates. Let such devotion, reverence and love permeate your Universities, your public and private life and everything which you undertake, you need not then clamour for political privileges, for there is no power on earth that could deny you them.

If you would see that true artistic spirit once more grow and spread, art must be ever present in your daily lives. The art you merely imitate cannot give it to you. It must come out from yourselves. It must not be only a thing you go to see in art galleries and museums. It must be something for daily use—something you see in the life which is round about you, in the streets and in your houses, in the trees and in the flowers, in the fields and in the sky—and something of the divine nature that is within you revealing to you thoughts divine. You must regard the books which you read only as commentaries on the great book of nature. You must go, as your Rishis did of old, and learn from nature herself. Nature will teach you many things which are not to be found in text-books nor within the dingy walls of your college class-rooms.

Indian art will then again become a great intellectual and moral force which will stimulate every form of activity. It will relight the lamp of Indian learning, revive your architecture, your industries and your commerce, and give a higher motive for every work you find to do. Your art, thus ennobled, will not fail to ennoble yourselves.